HEWLETT PACKARD

UNIVERSITY BUSINESS SERIES

$900

29488

CASES IN COMPUTER AND
MODEL-ASSISTED MARKETING: PLANNING

BY
George S. Day
GRADUATE SCHOOL OF BUSINESS
UNIVERSITY OF TORONTO

Gerald J. Eskin
COLLEGE OF BUSINESS ADMINISTRATION
UNIVERSITY OF IOWA

David B. Montgomery
GRADUATE SCHOOL OF BUSINESS
STANFORD UNIVERSITY

and

Charles B. Weinberg
GRADUATE SCHOOL OF BUSINESS
STANFORD UNIVERSITY

The Scientific Press
THE STANFORD BARN
PALO ALTO, CA 94304
(415) 322-5221

The Hewlett-Packard Computer Curriculum Series represents the published results of a Curriculum Development project sponsored by the Data Systems Division of Hewlett-Packard Company. This project is under the directorship of Harold J. Peters.

This material was developed at the Graduate School of Business, Stanford University.

The programs included in this unit were developed on a Hewlett-Packard 2000F system in Time-Shared BASIC at the Graduate School of Business, Stanford University, with support from the National Science Foundation under grant number GJ617.

The Hewlett-Packard Company and the authors make no warranty, expressed or implied, and assume no responsibility in connection with the operation of the program material attached hereto.

Library of Congress Catalogue Number 76-48777

ISBN 0-89426-004-9

PREFACE

The Text. In the authors' view, one of the greatest pedagogical barriers in marketing education has been the dearth of case material relating to analytical approaches to marketing planning. This casebook is the first in the *Cases in Computer & Model Assisted Marketing Series*. Since its publication, other titles have been added to the series:

Eskin and Montgomery, *Data Analysis,* Palo Alto, CA: The Scientific Press, 1977 Impression.

Weinberg, *Management,* Palo Alto, CA: The Scientific Press, 1977.

In preparing the four cases of this volume, our objective has been to present important, realistic marketing problems that will challenge students. We believe that the students should be encouraged to work through the materials on their own, rather than being provided with a canned solution. We hope that the cases will contribute to a better understanding of marketing as well as models; better yet, to the integration of the two.

The Castle Coffee case uses an abridged version of J. D. C. Little's computer model & his "decision calculus" to help decide whether to increase its advertising budget for a product whose sales have slipped badly over the past decade.

The Nikoll Electronics case uses two bidding models to assess risk & expected return on alternative competitive bidding strategies.

The Concorn Kitchens case projects historical P & L statements, and allows judgement on projections, for the next five years. Elasticity estimates allow analysis of the P & L impact of alternative marketing mix strategies for two lines of grocery products. One product has matured, while the other has growth potential.

The General Foods - Maxim case employs a new product model (the Ayer Model) to analyze the market potential of a number of attractive new product marketing programs.

The 1977 Impression adds supplementary material and a new appendix on synchronizing quarterly & annual budgets to the Castle Coffee case, and miscellaneous corrections & refinements to the other cases. Most of the material presented in this volume has evolved over the past nine years from cases taught to MBA students at the Stanford Business School. Much of the material has also been used at the undergraduate level fiSan Jose State, Berkeley, University of Iowa) and in executive education programs in the United States and abroad.

The Programs. Ideally the cases should be used in conjunction with on-line versions of the accompanying computer programs, although all cases have been successfully taught without the computer. For such situations, sample printouts are provided in the text for each case in order to allow classroom "simulation" of computer use.1

All computer programs have operated in an apparently "bug-free" fashion at the Stanford Business School computer installation on an HP 2000 ACCESS minicomputer. Only minor modifications should be required to allow operation on other equipment. Program listings for the programs used in each case are provided in the text to facilitate a transfer to other equipment. Paper tapes or a magnetic tape of all programs run at Stanford can be obtained at a minimal fee by writing to the publisher: The Scientific Press.

The Teaching Notes. An 84 page volume of teaching notes contains, within its format of Synopsis-Approach-Discussion Questions for each case, an enormous amount of helpful supplementary material including: overviews of each case, teaching objectives and suggested class strategies, comments on discussion assignments, notes on the programs, sensitivity analysis, histograms, reprints of journal articles pertaining to material in the cases, and the authors' published article summarizing the first five years of their experience using the cases in class. Copies of the *Teaching Notes* can be obtained from the publisher: The Scientific Press.

George S. Day, Toronto
Gerald J. Eskin, Iowa City
David B. Montgomery, Stanford
Charles B. Weinberg, Stanford
February 1977

ACKNOWLEDGEMENTS

The authors are grateful to the Graduate School of Business, Stanford University, for its generous financial support in the development of these materials. The programs were developed with the support of the National Science Foundation under Grant Number GJ617. Some financial support was also provided by the Marketing Science Institute, Cambridge, Massachusetts. The assistance of our various research assistants is also gratefully acknowledged, as well as the critical reading of our graduate students who pushed us to improve earlier versions of the cases. We particularly want to thank the General Systems Division of the Hewlett-Packard Company. Without the generous support of Hewlett-Packard, these cases would not have become widely available. In addition to arranging publication, we would like to thank Charles Dixon, Jean Danver, and Brenda Mapp; and Christine Doerr, who ably edited the manuscript.

Finally, the authors would like to dedicate this effort to three colleagues who have contributed to these cases (see the acknowledgements before each case) and who are now active in the "real world": Dr. Henry Claycamp of International Harvester, Vice Provost William Massey of Stanford University, and Dr. Charles McClelland of Lex Computer Systems, Inc.

TABLE OF CONTENTS

CASTLE COFFEE COMPANY [1] (A)

In May of 1972 Mr. Adrian Van Tassle, Advertising Manager for the Castle Coffee Company, tugged at his red mustache and contemplated the latest market share report. This was not one of his happier moments. "Blimey," he exclaimed, "I've got to do something to turn this darned market around before it's too late for Castle—and me. But I can't afford another mistake like last year . . . "

Indeed, Mr. William Castle (the President and a major stockholder of the Castle Company) had exhibited a similar reaction when told that Castle Coffee's share of the market was dropping back toward 5.4%—where it had been one year previously. He had remarked rather pointedly to Mr. Van Tassle that if market share and profitability were not improved during the next fiscal year "some rather drastic actions" might need to be taken. Van Tassle recalled a remark about "a return trip ticket to Singapore" unless something good happened soon.

Adrian Van Tassle had been hired by Mr. James Anthoney, Vice President of Marketing for Castle, in the summer of 1970. Prior to that time he had worked for companies in the Netherlands and Singapore and had gained a reputation as a highly effective advertising executive. Now, in the spring of 1972, he was engaged in trying to reverse a long-term downward trend in the market position of Castle Coffee.

CASTLE'S MARKET POSITION

Castle Coffee was an old, established company in the coffee business, with headquarters in Squirrel Hill, Pennsylvania. Its market area included the East Coast and Southern regions of the United States, and a fairly large portion of the Midwest. The company had at one time enjoyed as much as 15% of the market in these areas. These were often referred to as the "good old days," when the brand was strong and growing and the company was able to sponsor such popular radio programs as "The Castle Comedy Hour" and "Castle Capers."

The company's troubles began in the 1950's, when television replaced radio as the primary broadcast medium. Castle experienced increasing competitive difficulty as TV production and time costs increased. Further problems presented themselves as several other old-line companies were absorbed by major marketers. For example, Folgers Coffee was bought by Procter and Gamble and Butter Nut by Coca Cola. These giants joined General Foods Corporation (Maxwell House Coffee) among the ranks of Castle's most formidable competitors. Finally, the advent of freeze-dry and the increasing popularity of instant coffee put additional pressure on Castle, which had no entry in these product classes.

The downward trend in share was most pronounced during the 1960s: the company had held 12% of the market at the beginning of the decade but only about 5½% at the end. Share had held fairly stable for the last few years. This was attributed to a "hard-core" group of loyal buyers plus an active (and expensive) program of consumer promotions and price-off deals to the trade. Mr. Anthoney, the Vice President of Marketing, believed that the erosion of share had been halted just in time. A little more slippage, he said, and Castle would begin to lose its distribution. This would have been the beginning of the end for this venerable company.

Castle's share of market had slipped badly during the past decade, although brand share had recently stabilized. A major concern of the Advertising Manager was the fact that the increased advertising budget he had obtained the previous year had been cut back in mid-year because of management's dissatisfaction with the results. In addition, it seemed vital to begin to increase Castle's share so as not to lose distribution.

The Advertising Manager of Castle Coffee is now faced with the problem of preparing and justifying an advertising budget for the coming fiscal year.

---

[1] This case was prepared as a basis for class discussion. It does not depict an actual company. The text and computer programs were developed by Professors William F. Massy, David B. Montgomery, and Charles B. Weinberg.

OPERATION BREAKOUT

When William Castle was elevated to the presidency in 1968, his main objective was to halt the decline in market position and, if possible, to effect a turnaround. His success in achieving the first objective has already been noted. However, both he and Anthoney agreed that the same strategy, i.e., intensive consumer and trade promotion, would not succeed in winning back any appreciable proportion of the lost market share.

Both men believed that it would be necessary to increase consumer awareness of the Castle brand and develop more favorable attitudes about it if market position were to be improved. This could only be done through advertising. Since the company produced a quality product (it was noticeably richer and more aromatic than many competing coffees), it appeared that a strategy of increasing advertising weight might stand some chance of success. A search for an advertising manager was initiated, which culminated in the hiring of Adrian Van Tassle.

After a period of familiarizing himself with the Castle Company and the American coffee market and advertising scene, Van Tassle began developing a plan to revitalize Castle's advertising program. First, he "released" the company's current advertising agency and requested proposals from a number of others interested in obtaining the account. While it was generally understood that the amount of advertising would increase somewhat, the heaviest emphasis was on the kind of appeal and copy execution to be used. Both the company and the various agencies agreed that nearly all the advertising weight should go into spot television. Network sponsorship was difficult because of the regional character of Castle's markets, and no other medium could match TV's impact for a product like coffee. (There is a great deal of newspaper advertising for coffee, but this is usually placed by retailers under an advertising allowance arrangement with the manufacturer. Castle included such expenditures in its promotional budget rather than as an advertising expense.)

The team from Aardvark Associates, Inc., won the competition with an advertising program built around the theme, *"Only a Castle is fit for a king or a queen."* The new agency recommended that a 30% increase in the quarterly advertising budget be approved, in order to give the new program a fair trial. After considerable negotiation with Messrs. Castle and Anthoney, and further discussion with the agency, Van Tassle decided to compromise on a 20% increase. The new campaign was to start in the autumn of 1971, which was the second quarter of the company's 1972 fiscal year (the fiscal year started July 1, 1971 and would end June 30, 1972.) It was dubbed "operation breakout."

PERFORMANCE DURING FISCAL 1972

Castle had been advertising at an average rate of $1.0 million per quarter for the last several years. Given current levels of promotional expenditures, this was regarded as sufficient to maintain market share at about its current level of 5.4%. Castle's annual expenditure of $4 million represented somewhat more than 5.4% of industry advertising, though exact figures about competitors' expenditures on ground coffee were difficult to obtain. This relation was regarded as normal, since private brands accounted for a significant fraction of the market and these received little or no advertising. Neither Mr. Van Tassle nor Mr. Anthoney anticipated that competitive expenditures would change much during the next few years regardless of any increase in Castle's advertising.

Advertising of ground coffee followed a regular seasonal pattern, which approximated the seasonal variation of industry sales. The relevant figures are presented in Table 1. Total ground coffee sales in Castle's market area averaged 22 million cases per quarter and were expected to remain at that level for several years. Each case contained 12 pounds of coffee in one, two, or three pound containers. Consumption in winter was about 15% above the yearly average, while in summer the volume was down by 15%.

Table 1. Industry Sales and Castle's Advertising Budget

Quarter	Industry Sales		Maintenance Advertising		Planned Adv for FY 1972	
	Cases*	Index	Dollars*	Index	Dollars*	% Increase
1 Summer	18.7	0.85	.8	0.80	.8	0%
2 Autumn	22.0	1.00	1.0	1.00	1.2	20%
3 Winter	25.3	1.15	1.2	1.20	1.44	20%
4 Spring	22.0	1.00	1.0	1.00	1.2	20%
Average	22.0	1.00	1.0	1.00	1.16	16%

*In millions.

Advertising expenditures by both Castle and the industry in general followed the same basic pattern, except that the seasonal variation was between 80% and 120%—somewhat greater than the variation in sales. The "maintenance" expenditures on advertising, shown in Table 1, was what the company believed it had to spend to maintain its "normal" 5.4% of the market in each quarter. Van Tassle had wondered whether this was the right seasonal advertising pattern for Castle, given its small percentage of the market, but decided to stay with it during fiscal 1972. Therefore, the 20% planned increase in quarterly advertising rates was simply added to the "sustaining" amount for each quarter, beginning in the second quarter of the year. The planned expenditures for fiscal 1972 are also shown in Table 1.

In speaking with Mr. Castle and Jim Anthoney about the proposed changes in the advertising program, Mr. Van Tassle had indicated that he expected to increase market share to 6% or perhaps a little more. This sounded pretty good to Mr. Castle, especially after he had consulted with the company's controller. Exhibit 1 presents the controller's memorandum on the advertising budget increase.

Mr. Van Tassle had, of course, indicated that the hoped for six percent share was not a "sure thing" and, in any case, that it might take more than one quarter before the full effects of the new advertising program would be felt.

The new advertising campaign broke as scheduled on October 1, 1971, the first day of the second quarter of the fiscal year. Adrian Van Tassle was somewhat disappointed in the commercials prepared by the Aardvark agency and a little apprehensive about the early reports from the field. The bi-monthly store audit report of market share for September-October showed only a fractional increase in share over the 5.4% of the previous period. Nevertheless, Van Tassle thought that, given a little time, things would work out and that the campaign would eventually reach its objective.

The November-December market share report was received in mid-January. It showed Castle's share of the market to be 5.6%. On January 21, 1972, Mr. Van Tassle received a carbon copy of the memorandum in Exhibit 2.

EXHIBIT 1

August 1, 1971

CONFIDENTIAL

Memo to: W. Castle, President

From: I. Figure, Controller

Subject: Proposed 20% Increase in Advertising

I think that Adrian's proposal to increase advertising by 20% (from a quarterly rate of $1.0 million to one of $1.2 million) is a good idea. He predicts that a market share of 6.0 percent will be achieved, compared to our current 5.4 percent. I can't comment about the feasibility of this assumption: that's Adrian's business and I presume he knows what he's doing. I can tell you, however, that such a result would be highly profitable.

As you know, the wholesale price of coffee has been running about $8.60 per twelve-pound case. Deducting our average retail advertising and promotional allowance of $0.80 per case, and our variable costs of production and distribution of $5.55 per case, leaves an average gross contribution to fixed costs and profit of $2.25 per case. Figuring a total market of about 22 million cases per quarter and a share change of from 0.054 to 0.060 (a 0.006 increase), we would have the following increase in gross contribution:

$$\text{change in gross contribution} \quad = \quad \$2.25 \times 22 \text{ million}$$

$$\times .006 = \$0.30 \text{ million}$$

Subtracting the change in advertising expense due to the new program and then dividing by this same quantity gives what can be called the *advertising payout rate:*

$$\frac{\text{Advertising}}{\text{payout rate}} = \frac{\text{change in gross contribution} - \text{change in adv. expense}}{\text{change in adv. expense}}$$

$$= \frac{\$0.10 \text{ million}}{\$0.20 \text{ million}} = .50$$

That is, we can expect to make $.50 in net contribution for each extra dollar spent on advertising. You can see that as long as this quantity is greater than zero (at which point the extra gross contribution just pays for the extra advertising), increasing our advertising is a good deal.

I think Adrian has a good thing going here, and my recommendation is to go ahead. Incidentally, the extra funds we should generate in net contribution (after advertising expense is deducted) should help to relieve the cash flow bind which I mentioned last week. Perhaps we will be able to maintain the quarterly dividend after all.

I.F.

EXHIBIT 2

January 20, 1972

Memo to: W. Castle, President

From: I. Figure, Controller

Subject: Failure of Advertising Program

I am most alarmed at our failure to achieve the market share target projected by Mr. A. Van Tassle. The 0.2 point increase in market share achieved in November-December is not sufficient to return the cost of the increased advertising. Ignoring the month of October, which obviously represents a start-up period, a 0.2 point increase in share generates only $100,000 in extra gross contribution on a quarterly basis. This must be compared to the $200,000 we have expended in extra advertising. The advertising payout rate is thus only −0.50: much less than the break-even point.

I know Mr. Van Tassle expects shares to increase again next quarter, but he has not been able to say by how much. The new program projects an advertising expenditure increase of a quarter of a million dollars over last year's winter quarter level. I don't see how we can continue to make these expenditures without a better prospect of return on our investment.

cc: Mr. J. Anthoney
      Mr. Van Tassle

Private postscript to Mr. Castle: In view of our Autumn, 1971, performance we must discuss the question of the quarterly dividend at an early date.

I.F.

On Monday, January 24, Jim Anthoney telephoned Van Tassle to say that Mr. Castle wanted an immediate review of the new advertising program. Later that week, after several rounds of discussion in which Mr. Van Tassle was unable to convince Castle and Anthoney that the program would be successful, it was decided to return to fiscal 1971 advertising levels. The TV spot contracts were renegotiated and by the middle of February advertising had been cut back substantially toward the $1.2 million per quarter rate that had previously been normal for the winter season. Aardvark Associates complained that the efficiency of their media "buy" suffered significantly during February and March, due to the abrupt reduction in advertising expenditure. However, they were unable to say by how much. The spring 1972 rate was set at the normal level of $1.0 million. Market share for January-February turned out to be slightly under 5.7%, while that for March-April was about 5.5%.

PLANNING FOR FISCAL 1973

So, in mid-May of 1972, Adrian Van Tassle was faced with the problem of what to recommend as the advertising budget for the four quarters of fiscal 1973. He was already very late in dealing with this assignment, since media buys would have to be upped soon if any substantial increase in weight were to be affected during the Summer quarter of 1972. Alternatively, fast action would be needed to reduce advertising expenditures below their tentatively budgeted "normal" level of $0.8 million.

During the past month, Van Tassle had spent considerable time reviewing the difficulties of fiscal 1972. He had remained convinced that a 20% increase in advertising should produce somewhere around a 6% market share level. He based this partly on "hunch" and partly on a number of studies that had been performed by academic and business market researchers with whom he was acquainted.

One such study which he believed was particularly applicable to Castle's situation indicated that the "advertising elasticity of demand" was equal to about ½. He recalled that the definition of this quantity when applied to market share is:

$$\text{Advertising elasticity of demand} = \frac{\text{percent change in market share}}{\text{percent change in advertising}}$$

The researcher assured him that it was valid to think of "percent changes" as being deviations from "normal levels" (also called maintenance levels) of advertising and share. However, he was worried that any given value of advertising elasticity would be valid only for moderate deviations about the norm. That is, the value of ½ he had noted earlier would not necessarily apply to (say) plus or minus 50% changes in advertising.

Van Tassle noted that his estimate of share change (6.0 – 5.4 = 0.6 percentage points) represented about an 11% increase over the normal share level of 5.4 points. Since this was to be achieved with a 20% increase in advertising, it represented an advertising elasticity of 11%/20% = 0.55. While this was higher than the 0.5 found in the study, he had believed that his advertising appeals and copy would be a bit better than average. He recognized that his ads may not actually have been as great as expected, but noted that, "even an elasticity of 0.5 would produce 5.94% of the market—within striking distance of 6%." Of course, the study itself might be applicable to Castle's market situation to a greater or lesser degree.

One lesson which he had learned from his unfortunate experience the last year was the danger inherent in presenting too optimistic a picture to top management. On the other hand, a "conservative" estimate might not have been sufficient to obtain approval for the program in the first place. Besides, he really did believe that the effect of advertising on share was greater than implied by performance in the autumn of 1971. This judgment should be a part of management's information set when they evaluated his proposal. Alternatively, if they had good reason for doubting his judgment he wanted to know about it—after all, William Castle and Jim Anthoney had been in the coffee business a lot longer than he had and were pretty savvy guys.

Perhaps the problem lay in his assessment of the speed with which the new program would take hold. He had felt it "would take a little time," but had not tried to pin it down further. ("That's pretty hard, after all.") Nothing very precise about this had been communicated to management. Could he blame Mr. Figure for adopting the time horizon he did?

As a final complicating factor, Van Tassle had just received a report from Aardvark Associates about the "quality" of the advertising copy and appeals used the previous autumn and winter. Contrary to expectations, these ads rated only about 0.90 on a scale which rated an "average ad" at 1.0. These tests were based on the so-called "theater technique," in which the various spots were inserted into a filmed "entertainment" program and their effects on choices in a lottery designed to simulate purchasing behavior were determined (see Exhibit 3 on theater tests). Fortunately, the ads currently being shown rated about 1.0 on the same scale. A new series of ads scheduled for showing during the autumn, winter, and spring of 1973 appeared to be much better. Theater testing could not be undertaken until production was completed during the summer, but "experts" in the agency were convinced that they would rate at least as high as 1.15. Mr. Van Tassle was impressed with these ads himself, but recalled that such predictions tended to be far from perfect. In the meantime, a budget request for all four quarters of fiscal 1973 had to be submitted to management within the next week.

EXHIBIT 3

THEATER TESTS[2]

In theater testing, an audience is recruited either by mail or by phone to attend a showing of test television programs. When the members of the audience arrive, they are given a set of questionnaires, through which an emcee guides them as the session progresses. Usually, data on the audience's opinions and preferences regarding the various brands in the product categories being tested are gathered before the show begins. The show consists of a standard television program episode (or two or more such episodes) in which several television commercials have been inserted. At the close of the showing, audience members are again asked to fill out questionnaires, reporting on the commercials they remember, and are again asked to give their opinions and preferences concerning the various brands of the advertised products. In many cases, the members of the audience (or some proportion of them) also record their interest in the show as it progresses by turning a dial as their interest level rises and falls, which permits the analyst to trace "interest curves" for the program. One service, Audience Studies, Inc., of Los Angeles, also measures basal skin resistance continuously for some members of the audience, for recent studies have suggested that there is a connection between this measure and the audience's degree of involvement with the material on the screen.

The theater test is one of the most versatile of the available test methods. It can be used to test television commercials in many different stages of development, and it has sometimes been used to test radio commercials and print ads (presented in the form of slides). To offset the high cost of this method, several advertisements for non-competing products are normally

[2]From *Advertising* by Kenneth A. Longman, pp. 326–7 © 1971 by Harcourt, Brace Jovanovich, Inc. and reprinted with their permission.

tested in a single session, thus splitting expenses among several advertisers. The method yields fair measures of attention-getting power, credibility, and motivating power. However, it is not very valuable in diagnosing specific problems in the commercials. To some extent, interest curves and measures of skin resistance can help to pinpoint weak spots, but the best way to obtain information that will point the way to improvement is to hold a group interview session immediately after the showing, using a few people selected from the audience.

Discussion Assignment

1. State precisely what you think the objectives of Castle's 1972 advertising plan should have been. Were these the objectives of Van Tassle? William Castle? I. Figure?

2. Evaluate the results obtained from the 1972 advertising campaign prior to and after the cut in advertising funds. What do you think the results would have been if the 20% increase had been continued for the entire year?

3. What should Van Tassle propose as an advertising budget for 1973; How should he justify this budget to top management?

4. How should Van Tassle deal with the issues of seasonality and copy quality?

CASTLE COFFEE COMPANY[3] (B)

Since returning from a one-week management development course a few months before, Adrian Van Tassle had been working with Mr. Jack Stillman on the adaptation of a small "marketing planning model". Stillman was Director of Research for Castle, and quite experienced in computer models applied to a broad range of management problems. While he had little or no experience in the marketing area, he welcomed the opportunity to work with Van Tassle in this area.

The model being developed was an adaptation of ADBUDG II,[4] which had become well-known among the fraternity of marketing model builders. This model, which operates on a timesharing computer system, is designed to aid a brand manager or advertising manager to determine a reasonable advertising budget for his product. (An excerpt from Professor John Little's article, which describes the model in general terms, is included as Appendix 1.) ADBUDG II is somewhat elementary but definitely representative of the larger class of marketing planning or "decision calculus" models that were being developed during the early seventies (see Appendix 2). Van Tassle felt that it might help him clarify his own thinking, communicate better with management, or both. In any case, he definitely knew that he needed help in both of these areas.

THE MARKETING PLANNING MODEL

After reviewing the marketing planning model with Jack Stillman, Van Tassle asked Stillman to provide a list of the basic inputs required by the model. After much tugging at his red mustache and several conferences with Stillman, Van Tassle arrived at a preliminary set of estimates for the basic inputs. The input list and the preliminary estimates are presented in Table 2. Some of these factors were obvious, and many have been discussed already. (For example, see Table 1 in Castle (A) for the product class sales rate and seasonal index.) Only the ones relating to market share and the advertising plan itself required a lot of headscratching.

After the painful experience of the previous year's advertising budget cutback, the Advertising Manager is contemplating the use of an abridged version of J.D.C. Little's ADBUDG II advertising budgeting model. (See J.D.C. Little, "Models and Managers: The Concept of a Decision Calculus, "Management Science: Applications, April 1970.) The case provides some baseline judgments from Castle's Advertising Manager and presents the ADBUDG II model and Little's concept of a "decision calculus".

---

[3]This case was prepared as a basis for class discussion. It does not depict a specific company. The case and associated computer programs were developed by Professors William F. Massy, David B. Montgomery, and Charles B. Weinberg.

[4]See John D.C. Little, "Models and Managers: The Concept of Decision Calculus." *Management Science: Applications* Vol. 16, No. 8 (April 1970), pp. B-466 to B-485.

[5]The advertising planning model which Van Tassle used is an abridged version of ADBUDG II. ADBUDG II allows for a broader set of inputs, but some factors didn't need to be varied in the Castle situation and were programmed directly into the ADBG version which Mr. Van Tassle used.

Table 2. Preliminary Values for Inputs to the Advertising Planning Model (Annual Plan)

Variable	Preliminary Value
Number of periods	1
Reference market share	.054
Maintenance advertising per year (millions of dollars)	4.0
Market share at end of *year* if during the year:	
(a) No advertising	.027
(b) Saturation advertising	.10
(c) 20% increase in advertising	.060
Market share in long run with no advertising	0
Media efficiency	1
Copy effectiveness	1
Contribution ($/unit)	2.25
Brand price ($/unit)	8.6
Initial market share (the March-April result)	.055
Annual product sales (industry sales, in millions of cases)	88
Product price ($/unit)	8.6

Although Adrian Van Tassle had to develop a quarterly plan, he decided that the best first step would be to determine the size of the annual advertising budget. He felt that developing an annual plan would be relatively easier in that seasonal effects could be ignored and questions of how fast sales and market share respond to advertising could be postponed. In addition, he felt that the experience of developing an annual plan would sharpen his understanding of the model and his ability to use it.

After some thought Van Tassle concluded that, if his advertising were reduced to zero, he would lose perhaps half his market share in the first year. This would result partly from a slackening in consumer demand and partly from an accelerating erosion of Castle's distribution. If a zero rate of advertising were to be continued, he was relatively certain Castle would lose all its distribution, and hence market share. On the other hand, pushing advertising to saturation might nearly double the company's share. "Of course," he commented to Jack Stillman, "that figure could as well be .09 or even .11 or .12— we've never come close to blitzing the ad budget. But I don't think it could possibly be less than .08." He also believed that the most likely return on a 20% increase in advertising would be .06, though here again there was considerable uncertainty. Adrian still wasn't sure how quickly this increase would be observed, but he felt that this would surely occur by the fourth quarter after the change.

Stillman and Van Tassle had discussed extensively the question of how the model should be used. Among other things, they had both read a commentary by Professor Little on the subject (see Appendix 3).

Mr. Van Tassle had run the model using data that represented his plans as they had existed at the beginning of the 1972 fiscal year. The only deviations from the situation as it had actually appeared to him at the time (the late spring of 1971) were: (1) the previous period's market share,[6] which stood at 5.4% in the spring of 1971, and (2) the index of copy effectiveness for the autumn-winter-spring campaign, which he had recently learned was 0.90. (Curiously, the "old" advertising copy used in the summer of 1971 had been rated at 1.0.) Further, he now had judgments concerning maximum and minimum shares, a subject he had not thought about last year. The levels of brand advertising were the amounts he had planned for the year, not the amounts actually expended. Given the confusion with the media schedule caused by the abrupt cancellation of 20% of Castle's advertising weight during the winter quarter, Van Tassle doubted whether a run of the model with actual expenditures would be meaningful. The inputs and outputs for this run are shown in Table 3.

Table 3. Run of Advertising Planning Model Using 1972 Planned Expenditures

```
RUN
FADBG


INPUT WITH DATA STATEMENTS ?N
NUMBER ØF PERIØDS(MAX 10) ?1

REFERENCE CASE CØNDITIØNS
MKT SHARE AT START ØF PERIØD ?.054
ADV RATE TØ MAINTAIN SHARE (MM $/PERIØD) ?4
MKT SHARE AT END ØF PERIØD
   IF ADV REDUCED TØ ZERØ ?.027
   IF ADV INCREASED TØ SATURATIØN ?.1
   IF ADV INCREASED 20% ØVER MAINTENANCE RATE ?.06
MKT SHARE IN LØNG RUN IF ADV REDUCED TØ ZERØ ?0
INDEX ØF MEDIA EFFICIENCY ?1
INDEX ØF CØPY EFFECTIVENESS ?1
CØNTRIBUTIØN PRØFIT (BEFØRE ADV. EXP.)
EXPRESSED IN DØLLARS/SALES UNIT ?2.25
AVERAGE BRAND PRICE($/UNIT)?8.6
ØTHER DATA:
MKT SHARE IN PREVIØUS PERIØD ?.055
PRØDUCT SALES RATE AT START ØF PERIØD (MM UNIT/PERIØD) ?88
AVERAGE PRICE FØR PRØDUCT($/UNIT) ?8.6

BUDGET HØRIZØN CØNDITIØNS
CØNSIDER RESPØNSE TØ PRØDUCT CLASS ADVERTISING ?N
PRØDUCT HAS A SEASØNAL ØR ØTHER NØN ADV TIME EFFECT ?N
BRAND SHARE HAS A NØN ADV TIME EFFECT ?N
MAINTENANCE ADVTG VARIES?N
MEDIA EFFICIENCY VARIES ?N
CØPY EFECTIVENESS VARIES ?N
BRAND ADV RATE VARIES ?N
BRAND ADVERTISING (MM DØLLARS) ?4.64

ACTIØN CØDE :1=ØUTPUT,2=CHANGE,3=STØP

ACTIØN ?1


PERIØ SHARE   PRØDUCT      BRAND     CØNTR BRAND CØNTR CUMUL SLØPE
      PCT      SALES        SALES      BEF   ADV   AFT  CØNTR CC$/$
      UNITS UNITS DØLRS UNITS DØLRS  ADV  DØLRS  ADV
            (MM)  (MM)  (000) (000) (000) (000) (000) (000)
===== ===== ===== ===== ===== ===== ===== ===== ===== ===== =====
  1   5.94   88   757  5224 44923 11753  4640  7113  7113  0.41

ACTIØN ?2

CHANGE CØDE :0=NØ MØRE, 1=MAINT. ADV., 2=MIN. FINAL SHARE
3=MAX FINAL SHARE, 4=FINAL SHARE WITH 20% ADV ØVER MAINT
5=LØNG RUN MIN., 6=BRAND ADV.
7=REFERENCE  CASE CØND, 8=BUDGET HØRIZØN CØND
CHANGE ?6
BRAND ADVERTISING FØR PERIØD :
  1          ?4.32
CHANGE ?0

ACTIØN ?1


PERIØ SHARE   PRØDUCT      BRAND     CØNTR BRAND CØNTR CUMUL SLØPE
      PCT      SALES        SALES      BEF   ADV   AFT  CØNTR CC$/$
      UNITS UNITS DØLRS UNITS DØLRS  ADV  DØLRS  ADV
            (MM)  (MM)  (000) (000) (000) (000) (000) (000)
===== ===== ===== ===== ===== ===== ===== ===== ===== ===== =====
  1   5.70   88   757  5015 43128 11283  4320  6963  6963  0.48

ACTIØN ?3


DØNE
```

---

[6] At the beginning of fiscal 1972 (July 1971) Mr. Van Tassle did not yet have the results on the spring quarter market share.

Mr. Van Tassle next decided to test a quarterly plan. Jack Stillman indicated that some changes in the values of the variables would have to be made. Some were obvious: average sales rate per quarter is the annual rate divided by four. Other changes were more difficult. For example, if there were no advertising for a year, market share would drop by 50% (i.e., to 0.027) at the end of the year. Stillman suggested that market share falls off by quarter in the same way that a bank compounds interest—in this case at the rate of 16% per quarter. Thus, if there were no advertising for four quarters, market share would drop to 84%, 71%, 60% and 50% of the initial value. This seemed to be a reasonable approach, so Van Tassle let Stillman make the calculations which led to Table 4. He then made some trial runs of a quarterly plan—inputs and outputs are shown in Table 5.

Table 4. Changes in Preliminary Values of Reference Case Conditions for Inputs to the Advertising Planning Model (Quarterly Plan)

Variable	Preliminary Value
Number of periods	4
Maintenance advertising per quarter (millions of dollars)	1.0
Market share at end of quarter if during the quarter:	
(a) No advertising	.0454
(b) Saturation advertising	.0630
(c) 20% increase in advertising	.0554
Quarterly product sales (industry sales in millions of cases)	22

Table 5. Trial Runs of the Quarterly Plan

```
RUN
FADBG


INPUT WITH DATA STATEMENTS ?N
NUMBER ØF PERIØDS(MAX 10) ?4

REFERENCE CASE CØNDITIØNS
MKT SHARE AT START ØF PERIØD ?.054
ADV RATE TØ MAINTAIN SHARE (MM $/PERIØD) ?1.0
MKT SHARE AT END ØF PERIØD
   IF ADV REDUCED TØ ZERØ ?.0454
   IF ADV INCREASED TØ SATURATIØN ?.063
   IF ADV INCREASED 20% ØVER MAINTENANCE RATE ?.0554
MKT SHARE IN LØNG RUN IF ADV REDUCED TØ ZERØ ?0
INDEX ØF MEDIA EFFICIENCY ?1
INDEX ØF CØPY EFFECTIVENESS ?1
CØNTRIBUTIØN PRØFIT (BEFØRE ADV. EXP.)
EXPRESSED IN DØLLARS/SALES UNIT ?2.25
AVERAGE BRAND PRICE($/UNIT)?8.6
ØTHER DATA:
MKT SHARE IN PREVIØUS PERIØD ?.055
PRØDUCT SALES RATE AT START ØF PERIØD (MM UNIT/PERIØD) ?22
AVERAGE PRICE FØR PRØDUCT($/UNIT) ?8.6

BUDGET HØRIZØN CØNDITIØNS
CØNSIDER RESPØNSE TØ PRØDUCT CLASS ADVERTISING ?N
PRØDUCT HAS A SEASØNAL ØR ØTHER NØN ADV TIME EFFECT ?Y
INDEX ØF PRØDUCT CLASS SALES(REF CASE 1.00) FØR PERIØD:
   1        ?.85
   2        ?1.0
   3        ?1.15
   4        ?1.0
BRAND SHARE HAS A NØN ADV TIME EFFECT ?N
MAINTENANCE ADVTG VARIES?Y
INDEX ØF MAINT ADV (REF CASE =1.00) FØR PERIØD:
   1        ?.8
   2        ?1.
   3        ?1.2
   4        ?1.
MEDIA EFFICIENCY VARIES ?N
CØPY EFECTIVENESS VARIES ?N
BRAND ADV RATE VARIES ?Y
BRAND ADV (M DØLLARS) IN PERIØD :
   1        ?.8
   2        ?1.2
   3        ?1.44
   4        ?1.2
```

```
ACTION CODE : 1=OUTPUT,2=CHANGE,3=STOP

ACTION ?1

PERIO SHARE    PRODUCT      BRAND      CONTR BRAND CONTR CUMUL SLOPE
      PCT      SALES        SALES       BEF   ADV   AFT  CONTR CC$/$
      UNITS UNITS DOLRS UNITS DOLRS    ADV  DOLRS  ADV
            (MM)  (MM) (000) (000)   (000) (000) (000) (000)
===== ===== ===== ===== ===== ===== ===== ===== ===== ===== =====
   1  5.48    19   161  1026  8819  2307   800  1507  1507  0.44
   2  5.61    22   189  1234 10615  2777  1200  1577  3085 -0.19
   3  5.72    25   218  1446 12439  3254  1440  1814  4899 -0.49
   4  5.81    22   189  1277 10986  2874  1200  1674  6573 -0.70

ACTION ?2

CHANGE CODE :0=NO MORE, 1=MAINT. ADV., 2=MIN. FINAL SHARE
3=MAX FINAL SHARE, 4=FINAL SHARE WITH 20% ADV OVER MAINT
5=LONG RUN MIN., 6=BRAND ADV.
7=REFERENCE  CASE COND, 8=BUDGET HORIZON COND
CHANGE ?6
BRAND ADVERTISING FOR PERIOD :
   1              ?.8
   2              ?1.2
   3              ?1.32
   4              ?1.0
CHANGE ?0

ACTION ?1

PERIO SHARE    PRODUCT      BRAND      CONTR BRAND CONTR CUMUL SLOPE
      PCT      SALES        SALES       BEF   ADV   AFT  CONTR CC$/$
      UNITS UNITS DOLRS UNITS DOLRS    ADV  DOLRS  ADV
            (MM)  (MM) (000) (000)   (000) (000) (000) (000)
===== ===== ===== ===== ===== ===== ===== ===== ===== ===== =====
   1  5.48    19   161  1026  8819  2307   800  1507  1507  0.44
   2  5.61    22   189  1234 10615  2777  1200  1577  3085 -0.19
   3  5.65    25   218  1430 12295  3217  1320  1897  4981 -0.44
   4  5.61    22   189  1234 10615  2777  1000  1777  6759 -0.63

ACTION ?3


DONE
```

Mr. Van Tassle gave a final pull to his mustache, and turned to the evaluation of the results of running his model on quarterly data. He expected he would want to make a series of additional runs, including tests of alternative plans for fiscal year 1973, before making his advertising budget presentation and recommendation to management. He expected that use of the model would help clarify his thinking and lead to a better recommendation. He also hoped that the model would permit him to develop a better presentation so as to more effectively communicate his objectives and assumptions to management. He was not quite sure how to go about pursuing either of these goals, and he recognized he would have to develop his own methods of approach as he went along.

Discussion Assignment

1. Use the ADBUDG model to develop an advertising budget for fiscal 1973. (See Appendix 4 for instructions.) How should Mr. Van Tassle justify this budget to top management? Be certain to test the sensitivity of your recommendation to the assumptions you used in developing your recommendation. (Suggestion: first prepare an annual budget, then a quarterly budget.)

2. Using the ADBUDG model requires more documentation of assumptions and possibly more total effort than simply guessing about the "best" advertising level. Are the extra effort and computer costs worth it?

3. To what extent do you feel that ADBUDG satisfies Little's criteria for a decision calculus?

CASTLE COFFEE COMPANY (B) SUPPLEMENT

The analogy to bank interest compounding is not direct because the compounding has to be modified for persistence. This is shown in Appendix 4. This inclusion of persistence requires that Table 4 be modified as follows

Market share at the end of quarter if during the quarter	From	To
(a) No advertising	.0454	.0454084
(b) Saturation advertising	.0630	.0686375
(c) 20% increase in advertising	.0554	.0559092

Upon looking at the output in Table 5, Van Tassle was puzzled by the columns entitled "CONTR AFT ADV" and "SLOPE CC$/$." Stillman explained that slope and contribution measure two different elements. Contribution measures the results in only one period; however, advertising now may have an impact on future profits as well. For example, a fraction of the customers attracted to Castle coffee in one period by advertising may repeat purchase in future periods. The ADBUDG model includes this effect and the slope attempts to measure this effect by estimating repeat sales in future periods. In the quarterly model, this biases the quarterly spending pattern because first quarter expenditures have 3 periods to allow for carry-over but the fourth quarter has none. Stillman also remarked that the slope is a measure of marginal profits (marginal revenue − marginal cost). Stillman suggested that Van Tassle run the model over 8 or 10 periods, but only be concerned about the slope for the first 4 periods, using the same quarterly plan in the second and third years.

CASTLE APPENDIX 1 – STRUCTURE OF THE ADBUDG MODEL [7]

We seek a simple, robust, easy to control model of sales response to advertising. As a first step brand sales is partitioned into product class sales and brand market share. That is, we separately model what is happening to the whole industry or product class of which the brand is a part and what is happening to the brand's share within the class. Such a breakdown has a number of advantages, not the least of which is that marketing people usually think this way. Consider a given time period. We suppose:

1. If advertising is cut to zero, brand share will decrease, but there is a floor, *min*, on how much share will fall from its initial value by the end of one time period.

2. If advertising is increased a great deal, say to something that could be called saturation, brand share will increase but there is a ceiling, *max*, on how much can be achieved by the end of one time period.

3. There is some advertising rate that will maintain initial share.

4. An estimate can be made by data analysis or managerial judgment of the effect on share by the end of one period of a 50% increase in advertising over the maintenance rate.

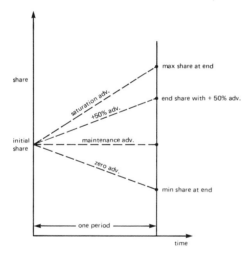

Figure 1. Input data for fitting a sale response to advertising function

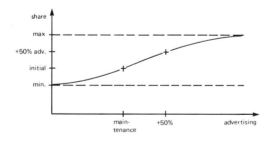

Figure 2. A smooth curve of share vs. advertising put through the data of form shown in Figure 1

---

[7] Reprinted from John D. C. Little, "Models and Managers: the Concept of Decision Calculus," *Management Science: Applications* (April 1970).

Figure 1 gives a pictorial representation of this information. The same data can also be represented as four points on a share response to advertising curve, as in Figure 2. A smooth curve can then be put through the points; for example, the function

(1) $$\text{share} = \min + (\max - \min)(\text{adv})^{\gamma}/[\delta + (\text{adv})^{\gamma}].$$

The constants *min, max,* δ and γ are implicitly determined by the input data.

Equation (1) represents a versatile but nevertheless restricted set of response relations. Actually I am willing to use anything. The curve could go down or up or loop the loop for all I care. It should be changed when and if a product manager wants it changed. Meanwhile, he can give four numbers, each of which has operational meaning to him and which together will specify a curve. It is doubtful that, as of today, we could specify a sales response curve in any greater detail than represented by a smooth curve through four appropriately chosen points.

I now claim that the above structure is robust. Suppose we do a two level spending test and run a regression that is linear in advertising in order to estimate response. Such a regression might make reasonable statistical sense but by itself would have absurd normative implications (advertising = 0 or ∞); it would not be robust. However, if the regression results are used to estimate the +50% point and a reasonable *max* and *min* are chosen we can expect reasonable answers. This would be difficult to prove in general, but with a specific manager and product it can usually be demonstrated satisfactorily by sensitivity analysis.

To be sure, more sophisticated models and data analyses can easily be suggested. A quadratic term could be put in the regression, for example, but its coefficient would almost certainly be unstable and normatively alarming. A Bayesian analysis or an adaptive control model like that of [3] might restore order, but the intellectual cost of such complications is high. Even if more sophisticated studies are done, they could probably be translated into a set of operational terms like the above. In any case we should start simply.

A person might well ask: Is the structure too robust? Conceivably a model could be so constrained that output would be almost decoupled from input. This is hardly the case here. The value specified for the share increase with +50% advertising is certain to be an important determinant of advertising rate. The values of *max* and *min* play the role of keeping changes in a meaningful range.

Incidentally, the sketch in Figure 2 shows an S-shaped curve. This is not required by (1). If $\gamma > 1$, the curve will be S-shaped, for $0 < \gamma \leq 1$, a concave function. The particular γ will depend on the input data.

A major omission in the description so far is consideration of time delays. To take these into account, the model assumes:

1. In the absence of advertising, share would eventually decay to some long run minimum value (possibly zero).

2. The decay in one time period will be a constant fraction of the gap between current share and the long run minimum, i.e., decay is exponential.

Let *long run min* denote the long run minimum and *persistence* denote the fraction of the difference between share and long run minimum that is retained after decay. Under the above assumptions:

persistence = (min – long run min)/(initial share – long run min)

(2)   share (t) – long run min = (persistence) [share $(t-1)$ – long run min]
$\qquad\qquad\qquad$ + (max – min) [adv (t)] $^{\gamma}/(\delta$ + [adv (t)] $^{\gamma}$).

This is a simple dynamic model. It is explainable and it behaves reasonably. It could be further generalized by permitting some of the constants to change with time, but that does not seem desirable at the moment.

But now what is meant by advertising? Dollars? Exposures? A product manager worries about spending rates, media, and copy. Let us construct two time varying indices: (1) a media efficiency index, and (2) a copy effectiveness index. Both will be assumed to have reference values of 1.0. The model then hypothesizes that the delivered advertising, i.e., the adv (t) that goes into the response function is given by

(3)   adv (t) = [media efficiency (t)] [copy effectiveness (t)] [adv dollars (t)].

The media efficiency and copy effectiveness indices can be determined subjectively, but better alternatives exist. Copy testing is helpful and data on media cost, exposures by market segment, and relative value of market segments can be used to develop a media index.

So far we have taken up share response to advertising, media efficiency, copy effectiveness, and share dynamics. Consider next product class sales. Two important phenomena here are seasonality and trend. These and any similar effects can be combined into a product class index that varies with time. Thus

product class sales (t) = [reference product class sales] [product class sales index (t)].

In addition there may be a product class response to brand advertising and corresponding time lags. The treatment of this is analogous to that for share.

A variety of other factors affect share and therefore indirectly or directly can affect the product manager's thinking about the advertising budget. Some of these factors are: promotions, competition, distribution, price, product changes, and package changes. These factors are all treated, but in a simple way, not unlike the way a product manager might handle them without a model.

Upon examining the factors, we find that the product manager has a definite idea about what various changes are likely to do for him. If he plans a promotion he does so with the expectation that something will happen to his sales and share. The same holds for a product change or price change. Therefore we ask him to construct an index of how he believes these factors will affect brand share in each period. The process can be formalized by filling in a table such as Table 1, listing all factors deemed by the product manager to be relevant. The composite index of nonadvertising effects is simply the product of the numbers in each column. Brand share will then be the product of the nonadvertising effect index and the share developed from the advertising response relation. For clarity the latter will be called the unadjusted share:

brand share (t) = [non adv effects index (t)] [unadj share (t)].

People often ask how product managers can make judgments like the above. The answer is that managers make such judgments all the time but in a less formal and less numerical way. Whenever they take an action they form some belief about what will happen. As a result, it has not proven difficult for them to make estimates which they feel reasonably comfortable with.

Essentially, the model is now specified. However, as we have added time varying effects such as media efficiency and the nonadvertising phenomena, we have created a problem for the inputs that determine share response to advertising. What values of the time-varying effects are assumed in the share response inputs? To deal with this question we introduce the concept of a reference case. The reference case is a standard set of values against which changes can be measured. The reference case includes a reference time period.

This is not one of the numbered time periods of the calculation but one set apart to serve as a standard. It can be patterned after a real period or can be constructed as a "typical" period. In any case each time varying effect is assigned a value in the reference period. From this data the sales response parameters *min, max,* γ and δ are then inferred.

TABLE 1.

Developing a Composite Index of Nonadvertising Effects

Index of Effect on Share	Period			
	1	2	3	4
Promotions	1.00	1.10	.98	1.00
Price	1.00	1.00	1.00	1.00
Package	1.00	1.05	1.05	1.05
Competitive action	1.00	.98	.95	1.00
Other	1.00	1.00	1.00	1.00
Composite	1.000	1.132	.978	1.050

To summarize the model:

1. *Share*
   brand share (t) = [non adv effect index (t)] [unadj share (t)]
   unadj share (t) = long run min + [persistence] [unadj share $(t-1)$ − long run min] + (max−min)[wtdadv(t)]$^\gamma$/{δ + [wtdadv(t)]$^\gamma$}

   wtd adv (t) = [media efficiency (t)] [copy effectiveness (t)] [adv dollars (t)] /r [reference value of numerator]

2. *Brand Sales*
   brand sales (t) = [reference product class sales] [product class sales index (t)] [brand share (t)]

3. *Profits*
   contribution to profit after adv (t) = [contribution per sales unit (t)] [brand sales (t)] − adv dollars (t)

The units situation has not been developed in detail here and we have omitted the effect of brand advertising on product class sales. . .

[One additional component of the model needs to be mentioned. It is an *output* item labeled CUM. ADV. Payout Rate (cumulative advertising payout rate).] This item is intended to answer the question that a user is most likely to ask: Which way should I change advertising to increase profit? But we must ask: What profit? Profit in that period or, since sales changes persist into the future, profit over several periods? We have chosen to anticipate the answer to be "cumulative contribution after advertising" in the last period of the calculation. But which advertising? We expect the question might be asked about advertising in any period. Thus we calculate

SLOPE (t) = the change in cumulative contribution after advertising in the last period, per unit change in adv dollars in t.

A positive SLOPE indicates that advertising increases will be profitable (in the above sense); negative, unprofitable; and zero, indifference.

The basic equations defining the model are really quite few. Nevertheless the structure permits consideration of share response to advertising, copy effectiveness, media efficiency, product class seasonality and trends, share dynamics, product class response to advertising, and a variety of non advertising effects such as promotion, distribution, and price. I feel that the structure meets the criteria of simplicity, robustness, and ease of control.

CASTLE APPENDIX 2-THE CONCEPT OF A DECISION CALCULUS [8]

If we want a manager to use a model, we should make it his, an extension of his ability to think about and analyze his operation. This puts special requirements on design and will often produce something rather different from what a management scientist might otherwise build. I propose a name to describe the result. A *decision calculus* will be defined as a model-based set of procedures for processing data and judgments to assist a manager in his decision making.

From experience gained so far, it is suggested that a decision calculus should be:

1. *Simple*. Simplicity promotes ease of understanding. Important phenomena should be put in the model and unimportant ones left out. Strong pressure often builds up to put more and more detail into a model. This should be resisted, until the users demonstrate they are ready to assimilate it.

2. *Robust*. Here I mean that a user would find it difficult to make the model give bad answers. This can be done by a structure that inherently constrains answers to a meaningful range of values.

3. *Easy to control*. A user should be able to make the model behave the way he wants it to. For example, he should know how to set inputs to get almost any outputs. This seems to suggest that the user could have a preconceived set of answers and simply fudge the inputs until he gets them. That sounds bad. Should not the model represent objective truth?

Wherever objective accuracy is attainable, I feel confident that the vast majority of managers will seize it eagerly. Where it is not, which is most of the time, the view here is that the manager should be left in control. Thus, the goal of parameterization is to represent the operation as the manager sees it. I rather suspect that if the manager cannot control the model he will not use it for fear it will coerce him into actions he does not believe in. However, I do not expect the manager to abuse the capability because he is honestly looking for help.

4. *Adaptive.* The model should be capable of being updated as new information becomes available. This is especially true of the parameters but to some extent of structure too.

5. *Complete on important issues*. Completeness is in conflict with simplicity. Structures must be found that can handle many phenomena without bogging down. An important aid to completeness is the incorporation of subjective judgments. People have a way of making better decisions than their data seem to warrant. It is clear that they are able to process a variety of inputs and come up with aggregate judgments about them. So, if you can't lick 'em, join 'em. I say this without taking away from the value of measurement. Many, if not most, of the big advances in scientific knowledge come from measurement. Nevertheless, at any given point in time, subjective estimates will be valuable for quantities that are currently difficult to measure or which cannot be measured in the time available before a decision must be made.

One problem posed by the use of subjective inputs is that they personalize the model to the individual or group that makes the judgments. This makes the model, at least superficially, more fragile and less to be

---

[8] Reprinted from John D. C. Little, "Models and Managers: the concept of Decision Calculus," *Management Science: Applications* (April 1970).

trusted by others than, say a totally empirical model. However, the model with subjective estimates may often be a good deal tougher because it is more complete and conforms more realistically to the world.

6. *Easy to communicate with.* The manager should be able to change inputs easily and obtain outputs quickly. On-line, conversational I/O and time-shared computing make this possible.

Every effort should be made to express input requests in operational terms. The internal parameterization of the model can be anything, but the requests to the user for data should be in his language. Thus, coefficients and constants without clear operational interpretation are to be discouraged. Let them be inferred by the computer from inputs that are easier for the user to work with. Expressing inputs and outputs as differences from reference values often helps.

On-line systems come through as being very effective in bringing the model to the manager. Some writers, for example Dearden [2], have belittled the importance of immediate response. They argue that decisions made once a year or even once a month hardly require systems that ·deliver the answers in seconds. Anyone who has used a conversational system perceives that this argument misses the point. Practically no decision is made on a single computer run. A person develops his understanding of a problem and its solution as he works on it. The critical time is not that of the decision deadline but of the next step in the user's thinking process.

Perhaps equally as important as the operational convenience of conversational programs is their contribution to learning. Good on-line models are user-instructing and introduce a person to the issues of the problem and the model much faster than would otherwise be possible. A person can rapidly get a feel for how the model works through direct experience. This is in sharp contrast to batch processing with its long time lags and imposing tribal rituals of punched cards, systems programmers and computer operators.

In summary, we are learning techniques of model design and implementation that bring the model to the manager and make it more a part of him. We are calling such a model a decision calculus.

CASTLE APPENDIX 3- APPLYING THE ADBUDG MODEL[9]

One might think that ways to apply the model would be obvious. Not really. The model has to be worked into the user's system. There are a number of ways in which this can and should be done. I shall describe one which we have just been through: The model was used to assist in the quarterly review of a brand plan.

The usual pattern of operations with a consumer product is to construct a brand plan. This is done once a year. The plan lays out the whole marketing program in considerable detail. However, as the year progresses and various parts of the program are carried out, changes get made: new opportunities arise, actual results come in and are not quite as expected, and generally a variety of unforseen circumstances occur. Consequently, a series of review and replanning points are scheduled, usually quarterly. This does not preclude actions at other times, which in fact take place, but it does at least schedule times in which changes are definitely considered or, if already made, are consolidated in a revised forcast of results.

Our goals in applying the model were to start from a "brand plan" view of the market, modify it to accomodate the new information contained in year-to-date results, then evaluate new strategies and repredict future outcomes. Here is what we did:

1. *Setting up the model according to the annual brand plan.* A set of input data was developed which would reproduce as model output the results found in the original brand plan. (If the brand plan has been constructed using the model, this step would not have been necessary.) The product class was identified. The seasonality and trends in product class were worked out. The input data for sales response to advertising was estimated by a combination of judgment and the examination of past time series of advertising and sales data. (In this case there were no spending levels test data but one of the side consequences of our study is that the company is seriously considering such tests for the future.) A promotion was planned for the second quarter and estimated to have a certain effect on share. A copy test, using two different areas of the country, was under way. The brand plan proposed that the test be continued for the year and so the copy index was held constant at 1.0. Similarly no substantial media changes were anticipated and the media efficiency was held at 1.0. A certain set of spending rates for advertising was envisaged and they were put into the model. A package and price change was under consideration but it had not gone into the plan.

   The assembled data was put into the model and fine adjustments were made in the parameters until the model predicted the brand plan results exactly. We then took the model as a reasonable indication of the product manager's feelings about how the market worked as of the time the brand plan was written.

2. *Updating the model on the basis of year-to-date results.* Our analysis was done after the first quarter data were in. Two principal events had occurred. First of all, sales were off from their forecast value. Second, media expenditures had been lower than originally planned. The first question to be asked was whether the lower sales could be attributed to the decreased media expenditures. Therefore, we ran the model with the new first quarter's advertising level. According to the model, the change would account for some but not all of the sales differences. The question

---

[9] Reprinted from John D. C. Little, "Models and Managers: the concept of Decision Calculus," *Management Science: Applications* April 1970).

then arose whether the advertising had a greater effect on sales than we originally thought or whether some other factors were causing sales to be off. The product manager's opinion was that other factors were probably responsible. The next question was whether the factors would continue to operate and he felt that there was no reason to believe otherwise.

Consequently we adjusted the nonadvertising effects index to account for the loss in sales observed in the first quarter and not otherwise attributed to the advertising decrease. The same adjustment was then continued through the year.

At this point it was possible to rerun the brand plan with the new parameters. It put forth a rather pessimistic view of the year.

3. *Evaluation of new strategies.* In the meantime, a number of new strategies had been proposed. First of all, because of the lower sales in the first quarter and the implied poorer profit position, the advertising levels for the rest of the year had been reduced. Secondly, the package and price change under consideration had been decided upon and was scheduled to begin in the third quarter. In support of that, the trade promotion was changed from the second quarter to the third quarter. Finally, more results were available on the copy test and a sufficient difference had shown up between the two areas that it was planned to implement the better one nationally in the fourth quarter. An estimate of the effect of the new copy on the copy index was made using the results of the test.

All these changes were made to the input. Furthermore a rough brand plan for the following year was put into the analysis. Then the new plan was run. This suggested there would be a substantial improvement in sales and profit compared to the previous case. It also showed that certain reallocations of advertising spending during the year and certain changes in the budget might well be warranted.

4. *Predictions of future results.* After the above runs were made a few further adjustments to strategy were decided upon. Thus the whole plan was run again. This run then became part of the quarterly review.

The above application illustrates the general way we expect the model to enter into the product manager's operation. However, each application is somewhat different. The previous one was very much of a team operation with the product manager being supported by specialists with marketing research and operations research skills. Although this is usually to be expected, in another case the product manager has run the model and made his recommendations almost single-handed. He found that it took two or three concentrated exposures to the model to become comfortable with it. In between he was pulled away by the press of other activities for a month or so at a time. Finally, however, he was confronted by a specific budgeting problem and sat down to work with the model intensively. Out of this effort came a report and a specific set of budget recommendations. His particular concern was the conflict between a strategy of budget cutting, short range profit taking, and possible erosion of market position and a strategy of maintaining or increasing budgets to try to protect or build share. He worked out sets of assumptions about market behavior and alternative company actions and, using the model, traced out their projected consequences. Finally he wrote it up with his recommendations.

The following conversation then took place between himself and his boss, the group product manager. They went over the report at length and, finally the group manager said, "All right, I understand what the model says, but what do you *really* think?

This is a good question because it uncovers certain important issues. First, has product manager lost control, i.e., does the model really reflect his view of the market? Second, the question may contain some implications that product manager is using the model in a partisan way to make a case for a particular position. Third, has the next level of management lost any control when the product manager's case is buttressed by this new tool?

The product manager was a little surprised by the question but his answer was: "*This* is what I really think. I've spent a lot of time considering the assumptions and results and feel they express my view of the market." As for the issue of whether the report might be partisan, it must be remembered that the product manager system is an advocate system, i.e., each man is supposed to look out for his own brand. It appears, however, the use of models may temper this partisanship because assumptions and data are explicit and subject to examination and relatively easy consideration of alternatives. For the same reason, although the next and higher levels of management need to understand the basis model ideas, once this is accomplished, the explicitness of the model and its inputs can actually make communications between levels more effective.

CASTLE APPENDIX 4 - SYNCHRONIZING QUARTERLY AND ANNUAL BUDGETS *

This appendix summarizes the problem of synchronizing quarterly and annual budgets. Here synchronizing means getting the same market share at the end of the year in an annual budget as at the end of the fourth quarter in a pro-rated quarterly budget. Because of the timing effect, the contribution will not agree.

The analysis in this appendix assumes that the long run minimum under no advertising is zero, and that the annual advertising budget is allocated in proportion to the quarterly maintenance level.

Using equation (2) in Appendix 1 with the assumption that long run min = 0, gives

$$\text{share } (t) = [\text{persistence}][\text{share } (t - 1)] + f(W_t)$$

where W_t is normalized brand advertising during period t and

$$f(W_t) = (\text{max-min})\left(\frac{W_t \gamma}{\delta + W_t \gamma}\right)$$

Further define

$$P_A = \text{persistence on an annual budget}$$

$$P_Q = \text{persistence on a quarterly budget}$$

$$f_A(W_t) = f(W_t) \text{ on an annual budget}$$

$$f_Q(W_t) = f(W_t) \text{ on a quarterly budget}$$

Then, synchronization is achieved when

$$PQ = P_A^{1/4}$$

$$f_Q(W_t) = \frac{1 - P_Q}{1 - P_Q^4} f_A(W_t)$$

Van Tassle's assumptions are

$$PQ = (.5)^{1/4} = \frac{1 - .841}{1 - .5} = .318$$

---

* Based on material developed by Keneth Kobylenski.

CASTLE APPENDIX 5 - INSTRUCTIONS ON USING THE ADBUDG PROGRAM

INSTRUCTIONS

Inputs can be made using two modes.

1. *Input through conversational I/O:*

   Straightforward; just watch the units used.

   > *Shares:* in decimal (e.g. 2% = .02)
   > *Ad. Budgets:* in millions of dollars (e.g. $400,000 = .4)
   > *Sales in Units:* in million units (e.g. 300,000,000 units = 300)

2. *Input through data statements*

   The options are still made conversationally (see sample run), but the data statements should correspond. They contain the same data that would be entered by the keyboard, and in the same order, given the options chosen.

   Data statements start at line 5000.

CORRESPONDENCE BETWEEN LITTLE'S NOTATIONS[10] AND PROGRAM VARIABLES

Little	Program	Variable
s_t	S[t]	brand sales rate in period t (units/period)
h_t	H[t]	brand share in period t
c_t	T[t]	product class sales rate in period t (units/period)
$\bar{h}_t$	K[t]	unadjusted brand share in t
n_t	J[I, t]	non-adv. effects index in t

Brand share/response function

α	A9	persistence constant for unadjusted brand share
β	B9	affectable range of unadjusted brand share
γ	G9	adv. response function exponent for brand
δ	D9	adv. response function denominator constant for brand
λ	L9	long-run minimum brand share
w_t	W(t)	normalized brand advertising in t
e_{1t}	E(t)	brand media efficiency in t
e^*_1	E0	brand media efficiency reference value
e_{2t}	F(t)	brand copy effectiveness in t
e^*_2	F0	brand copy effectiveness reference value
x_t	X(t)	brand adv. rate in t (dollars/period)
x^*	X0	brand maintenance adv. rate
d_t	J(2, t)	product class sales rate index in t
$\bar{c}_t$	V(t)	unadjusted product class sales rate in t (units/period)

---

[10] Reprinted from John D. C. Little, "Models and Managers: the Concept of Decision Calculus" *Management Science: Applications* Vol. 16, No. 8, April 1970.

product class sales response function

$$
\left.\begin{array}{ll}
\alpha' & \text{A8} \\
\beta' & \text{B8} \\
\gamma' & \text{G8} \\
\delta' & \text{D8} \\
\lambda' & \text{L8}
\end{array}\right\} \quad \text{similar to brand share resp. function}
$$

Little	Program	Variable
v_t	V(t)	normalized product class adv. rate
$v*$	V0	maintenance advertising rate for product class (dollar/period)
m_t	C(t)	brand contribution per unit in t (dollar/unit)
p_t	not named	brand contribution rate after adv. in t
T	N	number of periods
σ_t	A(t)	cumulative contribution after adv. for periods 1 to t (dollars)
η_t	B(t)	rate of change of σ_T (or A(N)) with x_t (slope)

Additional variables in the program

Symbol	Variable
P1	brand price per unit in reference period
P(t)	brand price per unit in t
P2	product class price in reference period
Q(t)	product class price in t
R1 through R0	result variables for printing
Z1 through Z5	control variables
Z$	input string for conversational I/O

Inputs

M0	share at start of period (reference)
M1	share at end if zero advertising
M9	share at end if saturation advertising
M5	share at end if advertising is 50% above maintenance
L9	minimum long run share
T0 T1 T9 T5 L8	same as above for product class sales

DERIVATION OF PARAMETERS FOR THE RESPONSE FUNCTIONS

Response function for brand share (program notations)

$$
K(t) = L9 + A9 * (K(t-1) - L9) + \frac{B9 * W(t)^{G9}}{D9 + W(t)^{G9}}
$$

Special cases

Maintenance advertising   W(t) = 1

(1) $M0 = L9 + A9 * (M0 - L9) + \dfrac{B9}{D9 + 1}$

Zero advertising   W(t) = 0

(2) $M1 = L9 + A9 * (M0 - L9)$

Saturation   W(t) = ∞

(3) $M9 = L9 + A9 * (M0 - L9) + B9$

Fifty percent above maintenance   W(t) = 1.5

(4) $M5 = L9 + A9 * (M0 - L9) + B9 \left(\dfrac{1.5^{G9}}{D9 + 1.5^{G9}} \right)$

Solution of (1)(2)(3)(4)

$L9 = L9$ (input)

$A9 = \dfrac{M1 - L0}{M0 - L0}$

$B9 = M9 - M1$

$G9 = \dfrac{1}{\log 1.5} \, \mathrm{Log} \left(\dfrac{M9 - M0}{M0 - M1} \times \dfrac{M5 - M1}{M9 - M5} \right)$

$D9 = \dfrac{M9 - M0}{M0 - M1}$

ADBUDG PROGRAM LISTING

```
1    REM  ADBG:   AN ADVERTISING BUDGETING MODEL 7/23/73
2    REM   THIS VERSION WAS PREPARED FOR USE WITH CASTLE COFFEE (B)
10   DIM Z$[72],A[10],B[10],C[10],X[20],V[10],W[10],U[11],K[11]
15   DIM J[3,10]
17   DIM P[10],Q[10]
20   DIM E[10],F[10],H[10],T[10],S[10]
27   REM CASTLE COFFEE QUARTERLY DATA (TABLE 4) AT LINE 5000
29   PRINT
30   Z3=0
35   Z5=0
40   Z4=1
50   PRINT "INPUT WITH DATA STATEMENTS ";
60   INPUT Z$
70   IF Z$[1,1]="N" THEN 120
80   Z3=1
90   READ N,M0,X0,M1,M9,M5,L9,E0,F0
100  READ C1,P1,K[1],U[1],P2
110  GOTO 420
120  PRINT "NUMBER OF PERIODS(MAX 10) ";
130  INPUT N
133  PRINT
135  PRINT "REFERENCE CASE CONDITIONS"
140  PRINT "MKT SHARE AT START OF PERIOD ";
150  INPUT M0
160  PRINT "ADV RATE TO MAINTAIN SHARE (MM $/PERIOD) ";
170  INPUT X0
180  PRINT "MKT SHARE AT END OF PERIOD"
190  PRINT "  IF ADV REDUCED TO ZERO ";
200  INPUT M1
210  PRINT "  IF ADV INCREASED TO SATURATION ";
220  INPUT M9
230  PRINT "  IF ADV INCREASED 20% OVER MAINTENANCE RATE ";
240  INPUT M5
250  PRINT "MKT SHARE IN LONG RUN IF ADV REDUCED TO ZERO ";
260  INPUT L9
270  PRINT "INDEX OF MEDIA EFFICIENCY ";
280  INPUT E0
290  PRINT "INDEX OF COPY EFFECTIVENESS ";
300  INPUT F0
310  PRINT "CONTRIBUTION PROFIT (BEFORE ADV. EXP.)"
320  PRINT "EXPRESSED IN DOLLARS/SALES UNIT ";
330  INPUT C1
340  PRINT "AVERAGE BRAND PRICE($/UNIT)";
350  INPUT P1
355  PRINT "OTHER DATA:"
360  PRINT "MKT SHARE IN PREVIOUS PERIOD ";
370  INPUT K[1]
380  PRINT "PRODUCT SALES RATE AT START OF PERIOD (MM UNIT/PERIOD) ";
390  INPUT U[1]
400  PRINT "AVERAGE PRICE FOR PRODUCT($/UNIT) ";
410  INPUT P2
420  PRINT
423  IF Z5=7 THEN 2360
425  PRINT "BUDGET HORIZON CONDITIONS"
430  PRINT "CONSIDER RESPONSE TO PRODUCT CLASS ADVERTISING ";
440  INPUT Z$
450  IF Z$[1,1]="N" THEN 640
460  IF Z3=0 THEN 490
470  READ T0,V0,T1,T9,T5,L8
480  GOTO 620
490  PRINT "PRODUCT SALES AT START OF PERIOD(UNITS/PERIOD) ";
500  INPUT T0
510  PRINT "ADV RATE TO MAINTAIN SALES (MM $/PERIOD) ";
520  INPUT V0
530  PRINT "PRODUCT SALES AT END OF PERIOD :"
540  PRINT "  IF ADV REDUCED TO ZERO ";
550  INPUT T1
560  PRINT "  IF ADV INCREASED TO SATURATION ";
570  INPUT T9
580  PRINT "  IF ADV INCREASED 20% OVER MAINTENANCE RATE ";
590  INPUT T5
600  PRINT "PRODUCT SALES IN LONG RUN IF ADV RED TO ZERO ";
610  INPUT L8
620  Z2=1
630  GOTO 650
640  Z2=0
650  FOR I=1 TO N
670  E[I]=E0
680  F[I]=F0
690  J[1,I]=J[2,I]=1
695  J[3,I]=1
700  P[I]=P1
710  Q[I]=P2
720  C[I]=C1
730  NEXT I
740  PRINT "PRODUCT HAS A SEASONAL OR OTHER NON ADV TIME EFFECT ";
750  INPUT Z$
760  IF Z$[1,1]="N" THEN 870
770  IF Z3=0 THEN 820
780  FOR I=1 TO N
790  READ J[1,I]
800  NEXT I
810  GOTO 870
820  PRINT "INDEX OF PRODUCT CLASS SALES(REF CASE 1.00) FOR PERIOD:"
```

```
830    FOR I=1 TO N
840    PRINT I," ";
850    INPUT J[1,I]
860    NEXT I
870    PRINT "BRAND SHARE HAS A NON ADV TIME EFFECT ";
890    INPUT Z$
900    IF Z$[1,1]="N" THEN 995
910    IF Z3=0 THEN 960
920    FOR I=1 TO N
930    READ J[2,I]
940    NEXT I
950    GOTO 995
960    PRINT "INDEX OF NON ADV TIME EFFECT FOR PERIOD :"
970    FOR I=1 TO N
980    PRINT I," ";
990    INPUT J[2,I]
992    NEXT I
995    PRINT "MAINTENANCE ADVTG VARIES";
997    INPUT Z$
1000   IF Z$[1,1]="N" THEN 1020
1002   IF Z3=0 THEN 1012
1004   FOR I=1 TO N
1006   READ J[3,I]
1008   NEXT I
1010   GOTO 1020
1012   PRINT "INDEX OF MAINT ADV (REF CASE =1.00) FOR PERIOD:"
1014   FOR I=1 TO N
1016   PRINT I;" ";
1018   INPUT J[3,I]
1019   NEXT I
1020   PRINT "MEDIA EFFICIENCY VARIES ";
1030   INPUT Z$
1040   IF Z$[1,1]="N" THEN 1150
1050   IF Z3=0 THEN 1100
1060   FOR I=1 TO N
1070   READ E[I]
1080   NEXT I
1090   GOTO 1150
1100   PRINT "INDEX OF MEDIA EFFICIENCY FOR PERIOD "
1110   FOR I=1 TO N
1120   PRINT I," ";
1130   INPUT E[I]
1140   NEXT I
1150   PRINT "COPY EFECTIVENESS VARIES ";
1170   INPUT Z$
1180   IF Z$[1,1]="N" THEN 1290
1190   IF Z3=0 THEN 1240
1200   FOR I=1 TO N
1210   READ F[I]
1220   NEXT I
1230   GOTO 1290
1240   PRINT "INDEX OF COPY EFFECTIVENESS FOR PERIOD:"
1250   FOR I=1 TO N
1260   PRINT I," ";
1270   INPUT F[I]
1280   NEXT I
1290   PRINT "BRAND ADV RATE VARIES ";
1310   INPUT Z$
1320   IF Z$[1,1]="N" THEN 1460
1330   IF Z3=0 THEN 1390
1340   FOR I=1 TO N
1350   READ X[I]
1360   X[I+10]=X[I]
1370   NEXT I
1380   GOTO 1510
1390   PRINT "BRAND ADV (M DOLLARS) IN PERIOD :"
1400   FOR I=1 TO N
1410   PRINT I," ";
1420   INPUT X[I]
1430   X[I+10]=X[I]
1440   NEXT I
1450   GOTO 1510
1460   PRINT "BRAND ADVERTISING (MM DOLLARS) ";
1470   INPUT X[1]
1475   X[11]=X[1]
1480   FOR I=2 TO N
1490   X[I]=X[1]
1495   X[I+10]=X[I]
1500   NEXT I
1510   PRINT
1515   Z3=0
1517   Z$[1,1]="N"
1520   PRINT "ACTION CODE :1=OUTPUT,2=CHANGE,3=STOP"
1530   PRINT
1540   PRINT "ACTION ";
1550   INPUT Z5
1560   PRINT
1570   GOTO Z5 OF 1580,1600,9999
1580   GOSUB 1620
1590   GOTO 1530
1600   GOSUB 2310
1610   GOTO 1530
1620   B9=M9-M1
1630   D9=(M9-M0)/(M0-M1)
1640   A9=(M1-L9)/(M0-L9)
1650   Y9=D9*(M5-M1)/(M9-M5)
1660   G9=LOG(Y9)/LOG(1.2)
1670   IF Z2=0 THEN 1730
1680   B8=T9-T1
1690   D8=(T9-T1)/(T0-T1)
```

```
1700  A8=(T1-L8)/(T0-L8)
1710  Y8=D8*(T5-T1)/(T9-T5)
1720  G8=LØG(Y8)/LØG(1.2)
1730  Z1=1
1740  GØSUB 2110
1750  Z1=0
1760  FØR I2=1 TØ N
1770  X[I2]=X[I2]+.05*X0
1780  GØSUB 2110
1790  B[I2]=(P9-A[N])/(.05*X0)
1800  X[I2]=X[I2+10]
1810  NEXT I2
1815  GØSUB 2110
1830  PRINT
1850  PRINT "PERIØ SHARE     PRØDUCT     BRAND     CØNTR BRAND CØNTR CUMUL█
1860  PRINT "      PCT       SALES       SALES     BEF   ADV   AFT   CØNTR█
1870  PRINT "        UNITS UNITS DØLRS UNITS DØLRS ADV   DØLRS ADV"
1880  PRINT "                (MM)  (MM) (000) (000) (000) (000) (000) (000)"
1890  PRINT USING 1900
1900  IMAGE 11("===== ")
1910  FØR I=1 TØ N
1920  R1=100*H[I]
1930  R2=T[I]
1940  R3=T[I]*Ø[I]
1950  R4=S[I]
1960  R4=1000*R4
1970  R5=S[I]*P[I]
1980  R5=1000*R5
1990  R6=S[I]*C[I]
2000  R6=1000*R6
2010  R7=X[I]
2020  R7=1000*R7
2030  R8=R6-R7
2040  R9=A[I]
2050  R9=1000*R9
2060  R0=B[I]
2070  PRINT USING 2080;I,R1,R2,R3,R4,R5,R6,R7,R8,R9,R0
2080  IMAGE 2X,2D,2X,2D.2DX,8(5D,1X),2D.2D
2090  NEXT I
2100  RETURN
2110  P9=0
2120  FØR I=1 TØ N
2122  X3=X[I]
2124  X[I]=X[I]/J[3,I]
2130  I1=I+1
2140  U[I1]=U[I]
2150  IF Z2=0 THEN 2180
2160  V[I]=(V0-X0+X[I])/V0
2170  U[I1]=L8+A8*(U[I1-1]-L8)+B8*V[I]↑G8/(D8+V[I]↑G8)
2180  W[I]=E[I]*F[I]*X[I]/(E0*F0*X0)
2190  K[I1]=L9+A9*(K[I1-1]-L9)+B9*W[I]↑G9/(D9+W[I]↑G9)
2200  H[I1]=K[I1]*J[2,I]
2210  T[I]=U[I1]*J[1,I]
2220  S[I]=T[I]*H[I]
2225  X[I]=X3
2230  P9=P9+C[I]*S[I]-X[I]
2240  IF Z1=0 THEN 2260
2250  A[I]=P9
2260  NEXT I
2270  RETURN
2310  IF Z4=0 THEN 2360
2320  PRINT "CHANGE CØDE :0=NØ MØRE, 1=MAINT. ADV., 2=MIN. FINAL SHARE"
2330  PRINT "3=MAX FINAL SHARE, 4=FINAL SHARE WITH 20% ADV ØVER MAINT"
2340  PRINT "5=LØNG RUN MIN., 6=BRAND ADV."
2345  PRINT "7=REFERENCE  CASE CØND, 8=BUDGET HØRIZØN CØND"
2350  Z4=0
2360  PRINT "CHANGE ";
2370  INPUT Z5
2380  GØTØ Z5 ØF 2400,2430,2460,2490,2520,2550,135,425
2390  RETURN
2400  PRINT "MAINTENANCE ADVERTISING ";
2410  INPUT X0
2420  GØTØ 2360
2430  PRINT "MINIMUM FINAL SHARE ";
2440  INPUT M1
2450  GØTØ 2360
2460  PRINT "MAXIMUM FINAL SHARE ";
2470  INPUT M9
2480  GØTØ 2360
2490  PRINT "FINAL SHARE WITH 20% ADV ØVER MAINTENANCE LEVEL";
2500  INPUT M5
2510  GØTØ 2360
2520  PRINT "LØNG RUN MINIMUM SHARE ";
2530  INPUT L9
2540  GØTØ 2360
2550  PRINT "BRAND ADVERTISING FØR PERIØD :"
2560  FØR I=1 TØ N
2570  PRINT I," ";
2580  INPUT X[I]
2590  X[I+10]=X[I]
2600  NEXT I
2610  GØTØ 2360
5000  DATA 4
5010  DATA .054
5020  DATA 1
5030  DATA .045,.063,.0553
5040  DATA 0
5050  DATA 1,1
5060  DATA 2.25,8.6
5070  DATA .055
5080  DATA 22,8.6
```

```
5085   DATA .85,1,1.15,1
5090   DATA .8,1,1.2,1
5100   DATA .8,1.2,1.44,1.2
9999   END
```

NIKOLL ELECTRONICS, INC.[11] (A)

Nikoll Electronics, Inc., headquartered in Iowa, is a multi-divisional producer of electronics equipment. The corporation was founded in 1936 by John Forman, a graduate engineer with an interest in electronics. During its early years, the company survived by assembling various types of radio equipment for Midwestern manufacturers. Operations expanded substantially during World War II as the company obtained large amounts of subcontracting work, mainly of an assembly nature. During and immediately following the war, Forman changed the character of his firm in an attempt to develop a proprietary product. His first effort was an improved version of a high frequency radio receiver which one of his associates had designed. The "new" product was immediately successful and the profits enabled Forman to invest heavily in research and development. During the late 1940's and early 1950's the company successfully introduced a series of new products and, by 1960, sales had grown to almost $40 million a year. By 1965 the company consisted of three major producing divisions (Consumer Products, Radio Equipment, and Solid State) and several staff departments.

The Solid State Division's products were high quality, technically sophisticated electronic subassemblies and integrated circuits designed for limited, specialized uses, with about 75% of division sales going to the U. S. Government. The products were constantly changing and the division regularly worked near the state-of-the-art in either its product development work or its production methods.

The division was organized with four major departments—all of which reported to the division manager. In 1964 a Solid State Oscillator Department was added to the division.[12] This department was responsible for its own research and development, engineering, manufacturing, and marketing activities. Nikoll's market share for this product was estimated to be about 35 percent compared to 40 percent for the industry's largest producer, Standard Parts.

Because such a large portion of its sales were to the government, the Manager of the Oscillator Department, Ned Seymour, was constantly troubled by the problem of bid pricing. Competition was severe and he was often forced to bid on a variable cost basis—or even below—to secure some business. In 1965, Seymore asked Tom Moore, Director of Corporate Operations Research, to investigate the feasibility of preparing a model which would help in determining the price to bid on contracts.

In his preliminary work, Moore found that the oscillator subassembly group's cost on a job was often a function of the price bid. Thus, if a low bid was submitted and accepted, the manufacturing group worked hard to keep its costs down. Conversely, if a "profitable" bid had been accepted, the manufacturing group did not strive as hard to hold down its costs. Moore also determined that substantial variations existed between contracts and bids in the gathering and utilizing of marketing information concerning the customer's needs and the competitors' strengths, weaknesses, and probable bids.

Nikoll Electronics, a multi-divisional producer of electronic equipment, has developed a relatively simple competitive bidding model which provides their management with a tool to examine the likelihood of winning and the expected payoffs from alternative bids in bidding situations. The model allows for intangibles as well as competitive advantage/disadvantage.

An opportunity to use the model in a concrete bidding situation occurs when Nikoll has the opportunity to bid on several options on a large oscillator contract. The contract is quite important to Nikoll since it represents a substantial amount of business and the opportunity to gain and hold leadership for this type of product.

---

[11] This case and the associated computer program were written by Jean Mordo, M.B.A. candidate, Graduate School of Business, Stanford University under the direction of Prof. David B. Montgomery, Stanford Graduate School of Business, and Dr. Bud McClelland, Lex Computer Systems.

[12] An oscillator is a source of power used in technically advanced laboratory and field test sets. A test set might contain a series of oscillators, each capable of producing a signal over a given frequency range, making the set useful for checking the accuracy and receiving power of a piece of electronic equipment.

At the end of three months, Moore and other members of the Operations Research Group had completed the job of constructing and programming the model, which was called NIK 1. The actual construction consisted of two steps:

1. *Determining the Objectives of the Model.* In explaining this step, Moore stated, "It would have been possible for us to construct a model which best served the interests of the corporation, the product managers working for Seymour, and/or Seymour himself. We knew in advance that the objectives of these three parties were not necessarily compatible. For example, the corporation tends to set year-to-year objectives on return on investment, while product managers often become excessively concerned about winning or losing a particular contract. Seymour, on the other hand, tends to look at the long run—the next five years. He worries about getting enough volume to hold his research group together and to hold his manufacturing schedule fairly constant throughout the year, and also about getting a big share of the market." It was decided that, since the Manager of the Oscillator Department was the person who would ultimately accept or reject the model, it would be useless to try to sell him a model which did not meet his objectives. "Therefore, I asked Seymour what his own goals were relative to the operations of the division. We finally decided we'd try to construct a model which would be predicated on the long run, but which would show what would happen in the short run also."

2. *Determining the Bidding Process.* The bidding procedure in the Oscillator Department involved the representatives of several functional areas. Chronologically, the steps were:

   (a) The Marketing Manager for the department received a request to submit a bid.

   (b) He referred the bid request to a Product Marketing Specialist whose specialty was within the product line concerned.

   (c) The Product Marketing Specialist requested a cost estimate from the Accounting Department.

   (d) A cost estimator from the Accounting Department obtained from the Product Line Manager estimates of the cost of manufacturing the product, i.e., the cost data, both historical and estimated, that he could use to produce a bid. This bid was always based on full-cost-recovery pricing.

   (e) He returned this analysis to the Product Marketing Specialist, who prepared an analysis of the market to supplement the financial analysis.

   (f) These analyses were presented to the Product Line Manager. The Product Marketing Specialist and the Product Line Manager jointly prepared a bid which was submitted to the Marketing Manager for approval.

   (g) If the Product Line Manager and the Product Marketing Specialist could not agree on a bid, the Marketing Manager would resolve their differences.

   (h) If the contract to be bid was large or particularly significant for other reasons, the Division Manager approved the final bid. He also resolved any remaining disagreements or even changed the suggested bid to one which he felt was more appropriate.

DESCRIPTION OF NIK 1

The basic model represented an attempt to simulate the process by which an experienced manager prepared a bid. The probability of getting the contract if a given price was bid was of critical importance. By multiplying this probability by the expected payoff, the model showed the probable value of submitting a particular bid. Mr. Moore explained: "We repeat this process for many different bids until we find the optimum price, that is, the bid which has the highest expected value of those bids we are willing to submit. Naturally, we don't blindly accept what the model puts out. We know we can't describe all bidding situations in this one model; even if we could, the cost would be exorbitant. We submit the model's output to the department manager for further action. If his intuition agrees with the model, we'll have done a pretty good job. If not, either some factor has been left out of the model, or the manager is biased by some personal consideration. Once we determine what the problem is, the model's suggested bids can be accepted or rejected."

Inputs to NIK1

In its completed form, the model made use of four inputs. Table 1 shows a sample run.

Table 1. Sample Run of NIK1

```
RUN
FNIK1

COMP BID(MIN,MAX) ?4700,5800
COST,INTANG IF WE LOSE?4525,200000
STARTING,ENDING PRICES,STEP ?4700,5500,100
COMPETITIVE (NON-PRICE) ADVANTAGE,MIN,MAX ?0,0

PRICE        PROB.WIN       EXP.PROF       EXP.INTAN      EXP.BENE
4700         .977437        19499.9        -4512.62       14987.2
4800         .949298        29760.5        -10140.4       19620.1
4900         .898306        38402.6        -20338.8       18063.8
5000         .818182        44304.6        -36363.6        7940.98
5100         .707498        46376.5        -58500.4       -12123.9
5200         .571978        44013.7        -85604.5       -41590.8
5300         .428022        37815.8        -114396.       -76579.8
5400         .292502        29177.1        -141500.       -112322.
5500         .181818        20209.1        -163636.       -143427.


MORE PRECISION ?YES
STARTING,ENDING PRICES,STEP ?4750,4850,10

PRICE        PROB.WIN       EXP.PROF       EXP.INTAN      EXP.BENE
4750         .965715        24770.6        -6857.06       17913.5
4760         .962841        25794.5        -7431.72       18362.8
4770         .959772        26806.4        -8045.7        18760.7
4780         .956497        27805.4        -8700.66       19104.7
4790         .953008        28790.4        -9398.32       19392.1
4800         .949298        29760.5        -10140.4       19620.1
4810         .945358        30714.7        -10928.4       19786.2
4820         .941179        31651.9        -11764.2       19887.7
4830         .936755        32571.         -12649.1       19921.9
4840         .932076        33470.9        -13584.7       19886.2
4850         .927137        34350.4        -14572.5       19777.9


MORE PRECISION ?NO
ANOTHER BID ?N

DONE
```

The first input was an estimate of the most critical competitor's probable bid. Factors considered in preparing this estimate included the opposing firm's financial condition, the capacity at which the firm was estimated to be operating, its bidding history and the bidding history of the person preparing that firm's bid, the firm's estimated cost structure, its capacity to develop or produce the product involved, the firm's policies on long-run versus short-run gains, any unique rivalry existing between Nikoll and that firm, the firm's position in (or out of) the market involved, the price structure of the market (e.g., firm or deteriorating), and any other information relevant to the opposing firm's probable bid.

One or several people might prepare this assessment. Usually that person most familiar with the market would be the Manager of the Manufacturing Group for that product, and his counterpart would be Manager of the Marketing Department. Their estimates were quantified in the model using a probability distribution. A normal distribution was assumed for the competitor's bid; the minimum and maximum bids were identified with the mean plus or minus two standard deviations. This was equivalent to saying that there was a 95% probability that the bid would be between the given limits and that the probability of exceeding the upper limit was equal to the probability of being below the lower limit.

The second input involved an estimate of the amount of bias which the customer held for or against Nikoll or its products. To prepare this estimate it was necessary to determine the basis on which the contract would be let. A customer might be concerned about a number of factors including price, the ability of the supplier to meet delivery schedules, unusual technical characteristics of a product, the back-up service which a firm offered—or any of a number of other factors. These factors were peculiar to a customer and a contract.

This estimate was quantified in terms of a price handicap for the competitor. For example, a 10% competitive advantage meant that when Nikoll's prices were higher than the competitor's by 10%, Nikoll still had a 50% chance of getting the contract. This competitive advantage was modeled as a random variable, with a normal distribution.

The third input consisted of the production costs of the contract. An estimate of the labor and material costs was prepared by the Manager of the Manufacturing Group. He considered historical performance, learning curve effects, startup costs, equipment required, and all other factors which influenced his production costs. Overhead rates were allocated by the Division Controller.

The fourth input was the intangible cost associated with losing the contract. It was a rough estimate made by the Manufacturing Group Manager and the Marketing Manager. It attempted to take into account long-run effects of the contract such as the potential loss of profit that would be incurred if the competitor were allowed to win and the need to develop the necessary expertise to compete more effectively in the future.

The SSI Job

An opportunity for the Oscillator Department to reach its goal of becoming the leader in the solid state oscillator field arose in April, 1966, when Systems Suppliers Incorporated (SSI) solicited bids for a large number of oscillators to be used in laboratory test sets designed for the military. SSI received the contract from Redstone Arsenal at a time when SSI was reportedly in financial trouble due to low sales volume.

The contract was for 57 sets. Each set contained two separate oscillator units each of which required one oscillator subassembly for each of eight frequency bands: A, B, C, D, E, F, G, and H. Bids were therefore being solicited on 912 subassemblies (114 in each frequency band). In addition, bids were requested for a possible follow-on order should Systems Suppliers wish to raise the total procurement to either 1,200 or 1,600 units.

SSI did not restrict itself to one supplier for the entire contract. Bids were requested on several options so that SSI could split the contract if it wished. The options were:

Option Number	Frequency Bands to be Covered
1	A, B, C, D, E, F, G, & H
2	A, B, C, D, E, F, & G
3	H
4	A, B, & C
5	D, E, F, & G

Nikoll asked for and received permission to bid on one other option:

Option Number	Frequency Bands to be Covered
6	A, B, C, D, & E

Nikoll requested this option because it closely matched Nikoll's present capabilities and its market expansion plans. Option Number 6, therefore, was the option the company was most interested in winning.

Nikoll believed it held a technical advantage in three frequency bands (A, B, and C) amounting to a virtual monopoly. Standard Parts, Nikoll's only significant competitor, was known to have started working on these oscillator subassemblies, but had not yet displayed any capacity to produce or deliver in quantity any oscillators in these frequency ranges. In the past year, Nikoll had successfully marketed an oscillator at H-band, one which was expected to be extremely competitive in terms of the SSI contract. Nikoll did not have or plan to develop an oscillator at G-band, but at F-band an oscillator was in the final stages of development. At E-band, the company was preparing a pilot production run, while both Nikoll and Standard Parts had successfully marketed D-band subassemblies.

Nikoll believed it held a technical advantage on all oscillators from A-through E-band, and in H-band, because its products were magnetically shielded. Magnetic shielding was important to SSI because Redstone's specifications required close physical storage of the oscillators, a layout that might cause equipment failure if their magnetic fields interacted. It was known that Standard Parts proposed to overcome this weakness by lining the storage containers with magnetic shielding material. It was not known with certainty if this technique would work.

The Customer

Determining the basis on which SSI would award the contract was relatively easy. SSI had the reputation of making decisions which maximized short-term profits. In other words, they were thought to be willing to take a high risk of a long-term loss in return for a high assurance of a short-term gain. Price, therefore, was thought to be the key to obtaining the contract.

This situation operated to Nikoll's disadvantage because, in issuing the contract, Redstone Arsenal had specified Standard Parts oscillators rather than "Standard Parts or equivalent." This oversight on Redstone's part had probably occurred because Redstone copied SSI's specifications when the contract was written. Nikoll was not successful in attempting to get Redstone to change this specification. Although Nikoll might legally have forced Redstone to change the specifications, this would have created ill will which the company was reluctant to incur.

Redstone's oversight worked to both SSI's and Standard Parts' advantage. SSI told Nikoll it would be willing to purchase Standard's oscillators in all frequency bands despite the risk of technical difficulties and failure to meet delivery schedules because it knew it could escape any repercussions by maintaining it had exactly followed the contract's specifications.

On the other hand, Nikoll was reasonably sure that SSI did not really want to do this. Nikoll thought that SSI probably wanted to split the order, with Standard Parts getting Options 3 and 5 and Nikoll getting Option 4. It was also thought that Standard Parts would be determined to get as much of the contract as possible, since their market share had dropped substantially over the past two years. This contract was quite large, and the firm which got the contract would probably gain or hold a leadership position in the market for some time to come. The combination of these circumstances meant that the SSI job was a prize well worth seeking but one that would be difficult to attain.

Applying NIK1 to the SSI Job

Nikoll had a week to submit its bids for the SSI job. Given such short notice and the complicated nature of the costs, the uncertainties of the costs, and the interdependence of the options, Tom Moore had to act both very quickly and very prudently. Even though NIK1 was not ideally suited for bidding on the SSI job because it did not consider the interdependence between options, it at least already existed. Tom believed that by using NIK1 as it was and exercising his own judgment on the results, he could obtain some idea of what the optimum bid price on each option should be. If he had enough time, he would try to model more accurately the SSI situation itself.

After several interviews with Ted Seymour and other executives of the division, Tom gathered the data summarized in Table 2.

Table 2. Summary Cost and Bid Data

Option	Unit Cost	Intangible If we lose	Competitor's Bid/Unit Minimum	Competitor's Bid/Unit Maximum
1	$7,805	$200,000	$6,700	$9,400
2	6,500	200,000	5,800	8,200
3	1,385	—	900	1,500
4	3,225	100,000	3,800	4,700
5	3,450	100,000	2,700	3,100
6	4,525	200,000	4,700	5,800
7*	3,440	—	2,300	2,900

*Standard Parts Reacted to Nikoll's Option Number 6 by proposing to bid on Frequency Bands F, G, and H.

Discussion Assignment

1. *What should Nikoll bid for each option?*

2. *How "robust" is NIK 1; i.e., how sensitive are the results to the various inputs?*

3. *What do you see as the most critical shortcomings of such a model:*

   (a) in general?

   (b) when applied to a case like the SSI job?

4. *What modeling would you do if you had a few more days to work on the SSI job?*

NIK 1 PROGRAM LISTING

```
1    REM  NIK1 CØMPUTER PRØGRAM TØ ACCØMPANY NIKØLL ELECTRØNICS (A) 7/23/73
10   DIM Z$[72]
100  A1=.278393
110  A2=.230389
120  A3=.000972
130  A4=.078108
140  PRINT "CØMP BID(MIN,MAX) ";
150  INPUT A,B
160  PRINT "CØST,INTANG IF WE LØSE";
170  INPUT C1,I1
180  PRINT "STARTING,ENDING PRICES,STEP ";
190  INPUT P1,P2,P3
200  PRINT "CØMPETITIVE (NØN-PRICE) ADVANTAGE,MIN,MAX ";
210  INPUT Y1,Y2
212  M2=(Y1+Y2)/2
214  S2=(Y2-Y1)/4
220  M1=(A+B)/2
230  S1=(B-A)/4
235  M3=M1+M2
236  S3=SØR(S1*S1+S2*S2)
240  PRINT
250  PRINT "PRICE","PRØB.WIN","EXP.PRØF","EXP.INTAN","EXP.BENE"
260  FØR P=P1 TØ P2 STEP P3
270  Z=(P-M3)/S3
280  X=ABS(Z)/SØR(2)
290  U=1+X*(A1+X*(A2+X*(A3+X*A4)))
300  U=U↑4
310  U=1-1/U
320  U=U/2
330  Q=.5+SGN(Z)*U
340  Q=1-Q
350  X1=114*(P-C1)*Q
360  X2=-I1*(1-Q)
370  PRINT P,Q,X1,X2,X1+X2
380  NEXT P
390  PRINT
400  PRINT
410  PRINT "MØRE PRECISIØN ";
420  INPUT Z$
430  IF Z$[1,1]="N" THEN 470
440  PRINT "STARTING,ENDING PRICES,STEP ";
450  INPUT P1,P2,P3
460  GØTØ 240
470  PRINT "ANØTHER BID ";
480  INPUT Z$
490  IF Z$[1,1]="Y" THEN 140
500  END
```

NIKOLL ELECTRONICS, INC. [13] (B)

Nikoll Electronics started to study the SSI job in order to submit a bid. During the first three days, Tom Moore, Director of Corporate Operations Research, collected cost data and interviewed two of the division executives most knowledgeable about what Standard Parts' bid would be.

Using the NIK 1 model that had been developed for a much simpler situation, he had come up with some idea of what Nikoll should bid. He was, however, worried about several things.

First, the nature of the situation made the outcome of each option bid dependent on the outcome of all the others. In the NIK 1 model, raising the price on one option necessarily meant increasing the probability of Standard's getting it, while in this case it could mean increasing the probability of Nikoll's getting another option.

Second, not all costs were linked to the option to be manufactured; some, such as the intangible costs, were linked to the outcome of the whole bidding process. Getting no option at all is one outcome, getting two that are not mutually exclusive is another.

Third, an option's maximum and minimum bids were in fact derived in some way from the prices of individual bands and so had to be correlated in some fashion. Moreover, quotations on individual bands might or might not be correlated with one another.

With two days left before the deadline for submitting the bid and with at least the results of NIK1 to fall back on, Tom Moore decided to go ahead and model the situation in its actual complexity. The size of the contract was such that the whole future of Nikoll's share in this growing business was at stake. After two days and two nights, living on sandwiches and getting very little sleep, Tom came up with NIK2.

DESCRIPTION OF NIK2

The NIK2 model was designed to analyze the situation in terms of the global outcome of the bidding process, rather than the outcome of one option. The model followed the following steps:

1. Take as inputs: Competition's price for each option
   Direct manufacturing costs for each option
   Outcome-linked tangible costs
   Outcome-linked intangible costs.

2. Draw competition's prices from appropriate probability distribution.

3. Combine inputs and competition's prices to determine the outcome.

4. Accumulate number of times each outcome occurs.

5. Repeat n times Steps 2-4.

6. Print results.

In this case the Nikoll Electronics Company modifies its bidding model to better reflect the oscillator bidding situation. The revised model considers the fact that competitors bids on various options might be related. The model also considers the impact of winning various options on overhead billing arrangements on the government contracts.

---

[13] This case and associated computer program were written by Jean Mordo, M. B. A. candidate, Graduate School of Business, Stanford University under the direction of Prof. David B. Montgomery, Stanford Graduate School of Business, and Dr. Bud McClelland, Lex Computer Systems.

Further description of NIK2, plus a program listing, can be found in Appendix 1.

Outcomes

The bidding process could result in ten distinct outcomes.

Outcome	Options Won By Nikoll	Bands Won By Nikoll
1	#1	all
2	none	none
3	#2	all but H
4	#3	H
5	#3 and #4	A, B, C, & H
6	#5	D, E, F, G
7	#3 and #5	D, E, F, G, & H
8	#4	A, B, C
9	#6	A, B, C, D, E
10	#7	F, G, H

Costs

Costs were of two kinds: option-linked and outcome-linked. Option-linked direct costs were the direct costs of manufacturing each band.

Band	Direct Manufacturing Cost
A	$1,300
B	800
C	600
D	500
E	500
F	800
G	1,000
H	1,200

Outcome-linked direct costs of the contract were several. First, additional costs would be incurred if Nikoll had more than a certain number of bands to manufacture. Such costs would be due to the purchase of additional machinery to be written off during the contract; costs would also be incurred in training additional direct workers and in hiring additional indirect labor. The table below summarizes the direct costs of this kind:

Number of Bands Won by Nikoll	Additional Costs
1-2	$10,000
3	25,000
4-5-6	45,000
7-8	60,000

Another category of direct cost that was dependent on the outcome of the bidding process was what Tom called the "G-effect." This was a direct cost incurred because of the reallocation of divisional overhead away from government business each time a commercial contract was taken.

It was estimated that during the execution of the contract, expected to take one year, about $500,000 of government ("cost-breakdown") business and about $1,500,000 of commercial business would be booked, not counting the SSI job. The divisional overhead would be running at about $480,000. Thus, if the SSI job was not taken, the government jobs would be charged

$$\frac{500}{500 + 1500} = \frac{1}{4}$$

of the overhead. On top of that, Nikoll was allowed to earn a 15% margin on its costs, including overhead. Given the amount of the SSI contract, one could calculate how much of the overhead and margin thereon would be lost due to renegotiation of the price on government business. This is summarized below:

SSI Contract	"G-effect" Cost
$200,000	$12,500
400,000	23,000
600,000	31,800
800,000	39,400

The last category of outcome-linked costs was the intangible costs. They were estimated by trying to take into account the potential loss of sales and profit to the competition over several years. Nikoll had developed expertise in the top five bands and had an edge over Standard Parts and other competitors. Allowing Standard Parts to get the contract for any of the top bands would permit them to develop the capacity to compete more effectively with Nikoll in the future. Tom Moore, working with the Division Manager, finally came up with the following intangible costs:

Bands Standard Obtains	Intangible Cost
A, B, C, D, E	$200,000
A, B, C, but not D, E	100,000
D, E, but not A, B, C	50,000

All costs are summarized in Table 3.

Table 3
NIKOLL ELECTRONICS, INC. (B)
Summary of Costs

	Won by Nikoll		Won by Competition		Manufact. Cost $/Set	Additional Costs	$000 Total Cost "G-effect"	Intangible Costs
Outcome	Options	Bands	Options	Bands				
1	1	ABCDEFGH	none	....	6,700	60	66	0
3	2	ABCDEFG .	3	.......H	5,500	60	55	0
4	3	.......H	2	ABCDEFG .	1,200	10	11	200
8	4	ABC.....	3 & 5	...DEFGH	2,700	25	35	100
6	5	...DEFG .	3 & 4	ABC....H	2,800	45	29	100
9	6	ABCDE ...	7	.....FGH	3,700	45	49	0
10	7	.....FGH	6	ABCDE ...	3,000	25	25	200
5	3 & 4	ABC....H	5	...DEFG .	3,900	45	25	100
7	3 & 5	...DEFGH	4	ABC.....	4,000	45	46	100
2	none	....	1	ABCDEFGH	———	0	0	200

Discussion Assignment

1. What bid would you submit on the various options? Why?

2. How comfortable do you feel with the results of NIK 2?

3. How would you use these results?

4. Do you foresee any implementation problems?

NIKOLL (B) APPENDIX 1–NIK 2 COMPUTER MODEL

LOGIC

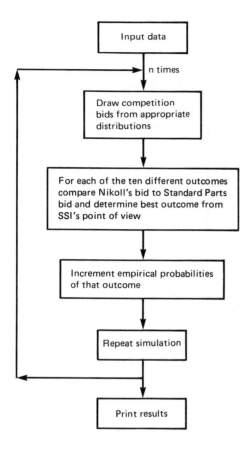

ALTERNATIVES

The program offers the choice to generate competition's bids for the various options either independently from one another or completely correlated. By this means some insight may be gained as to what would happen in an intermediate case.

In NIK 2 the options may either be perfectly correlated (i.e., the inter option correlation is 1) or perfectly uncorrelated (i.e., the inter option correlation is 0). A perfect correlation implies that if the competitor bids high (low) on one option he will bid high (low) on the others. Zero correlation implies that if the competitor bids high (low) on one option it does not affect the likelihood that he'll bid high (low) on any others.[14]

The program also has some convenient features such as changing the data on a conversational basis. Sample runs follow.

---

[14]Technically, the perfect correlation case goes to the normal random number subroutine only once and uses the results for each option. The zero correlation case goes to the normal random number subroutine once for each option.

```
RUN
FNIK2

ACTION CODE:1=RESTORE,2=PRINT DATA,3=RUN,4=CHANGE,5=STOP

ACTION ?2

CURRENT INPUT DATA
=================

              (DOLLARS PER UNIT)
=================================================
OPTION  BANDS    COMPETITION BIDS  MANUFG   PRICE
                 MINIMUM  MAXIMUM    COST
======  =======  =======  =======  ======  =====
   1    ABCDEFGH   6700     9400     6700    7610
   2    ABCDEFG.   5800     8200     5500    6490
   3    .......H    900     1500     1200    1460
   4    ABC.....   3800     4700     2700    3920
   5    ...DEFG.   2700     3100     2800    2830
   6    ABCDE...   4700     5800     3700    4830
   7    ....FGH    2300     2900     3000    4000

OUTCOME TABLE ?YES
              ($ THOUSANDS)
======================================================================
OUTCOME OPTIONS MANUFG ADDITL TANGIB REVNUE PROFIT INTANG   NET
        WE GET   COST   COST   COST                 COST  BENEFIT
======= ======= ====== ====== ====== ====== ====== ====== ======
   1       1      764    126    890    868    -22     0     -22
   2              0       0      0      0      0      200   -200
   3       2      627    115    742    740    -2      0      -2
   4       3      137    21     158    166     9      200   -191
   5      3+4     445    70     515    613    99      50     49
   6       5      319    74     393    323    -71     150   -221
   7      3+5     456    91     547    489    -58     200   -258
   8       4      308    60     368    447    79      50     29
   9       6      422    94     516    551    35      0      35
  10       7      342    50     392    456    64      180   -116

COMPETITIVE ADVANTAGE(MIN,MAX) : 0        0

INTER-OPTION CORRELATION 1

NUMBER OF ITERATIONS  100

ACTION ?3

EXPECTED PROFIT: 26.8686
EXPECTED INTANG:-26
EXP. NET BENEF.: .868603

WANT PROBABILITIES?Y

OUTCOME PROBABILITY
======= ===========
   1       0.060
   2       0.130
   3       0.000
   4       0.000
   5       0.000
   6       0.000
   7       0.000
   8       0.000
   9       0.810
  10       0.000

ACTION ?4
CHANGE CODE:0=NO MORE,1=PRICE,2=COMP.BID,3=OP.CORR.,4=#ITERAT.

CHANGE ?1
INPUT OPTION #,NEW PRICE ?6,4900
CHANGE ?1
INPUT OPTION #,NEW PRICE ?4,3820
CHANGE ?0

ACTION ?3

EXPECTED PROFIT: 23.539
EXPECTED INTANG:-14.
EXP. NET BENEF.: 9.53899

WANT PROBABILITIES?NO

ACTION ?4
CHANGE CODE:0=NO MORE,1=PRICE,2=COMP.BID,3=OP.CORR.,4=#ITERAT.

CHANGE ?4
INPUT # OF ITERATIONS ?500
CHANGE ?0

ACTION ?3

EXPECTED PROFIT: 21.0738
EXPECTED INTANG:-31.6
EXP. NET BENEF.:-10.5262

WANT PROBABILITIES?NO

ACTION ?5

DONE
```

NIK 2 PROGRAM LISTING

```
NIK2

1     REM NIK2 COMPUTER PROGRAM TO ACCOMPANY NIKOLL ELECTRONICS (B)
2     REM 7/24/73
3     REM THE DATA STATEMENTS ARE ORGANIZED AS FOLLOWS:
4     REM STATEMENT        1ST VAR. , 2ND VAR. , 3RD VAR. , 4TH VAR.
5     REM NUMBER
6     REM --------------------------------------------------------
7     REM    6000   DATA COMP.MIN., COMP.MAX., MFGR.COST, PRICE
8     REM                 OPTION1      OPTION1      OPTION1    OPTION1
9     REM       .       .        .        .        .        .
10    REM       .       .        .        .        .        .
11    REM       .       .        .        .        .        .
12    REM    6060   DATA COMP.MIN., COMP.MAX., MFGR.COST, PRICE
13    REM                 OPTION7      OPTION7      OPTION7    OPTION7
14    REM    6100   DATA ADDITL. COST OUTCOME1, INTANG.COST OUTCOME1
15    REM       .       .        .        .        .
16    REM       .       .        .        .        .
17    REM       .       .        .        .        .
18    REM    6190   DATA ADDITL. COST OUTCOME10, INTANG. COST OUTCOME10
19    REM    6200   DATA   COMP. ADVANTAGE MIN., COMP.ADVANTAGE MAX
20    REM    6300   DATA   NUMBER OF ITERATIONS IN THE SIMULATION
21    REM    6400   DATA   INTER-OPTION CORRELATION (MUST BE 0 OR 1 )
100   GOSUB 8000
110   DIM V$[56],W$[30],Z$[72]
120   PRINT "ACTION CODE:1=RESTORE,2=PRINT DATA,3=RUN,4=CHANGE,5=STOP"
130   GOSUB 290
140   PRINT
142   PRINT "ACTION ";
150   INPUT Z2
160   GOTO Z2 OF 170,200,230,260,280
170   RESTORE
180   GOSUB 290
190   GOTO 140
200   GOSUB 720
210   GOSUB 381
220   GOTO 140
230   GOSUB 720
240   GOSUB 1010
250   GOTO 140
260   GOSUB 4000
270   GOTO 140
280   GOTO 9999
290   FOR O1=1 TO 7
300   READ A[O1],B[O1],M[O1],P[O1]
310   NEXT O1
320   FOR K=1 TO 10
330   READ C[K],I[K]
340   NEXT K
350   READ Y1,Y2
360   READ NO
370   READ I1
371   IF I1=0 THEN 380
372   IF I1=1 THEN 380
373   PRINT "INTER-OPTION CORRELATION IS NOT EQUAL TO 0 OR 1 IN"
374   PRINT "DATA STATEMENT 6400"
375   PRINT "PLEASE RETYPE CORRECTED DATA STATEMENT AND THEN RUN"
376   GOTO 9999
380   RETURN
381   PRINT
390   PRINT "CURRENT INPUT DATA"
400   PRINT "=================="
410   PRINT
420   PRINT "               (DOLLARS PER UNIT)"
430   PRINT "============================================="
440   PRINT "OPTION  BANDS    COMPETITION BIDS  MANUFG  PRICE"
450   PRINT "                 MINIMUM  MAXIMUM   COST"
460   PRINT "======  =======  =======  =======  ======  ====="
470   FOR O1=1 TO 7
480   PRINT  USING 490;O1,V$[1+8*(O1-1),8*O1],A[O1],B[O1],M[O1],P[O1]
490   IMAGE 4D,3X,8A,3X,4D,5X,3(4D,4X)
500   NEXT O1
510   PRINT
512   PRINT "OUTCOME TABLE ";
514   INPUT Z$
516   IF Z$[1,1]="N" THEN 660
520   PRINT "               ($ THOUSANDS)"
530   PRINT "=================================================="
540   PRINT "OUTCOME OPTIONS MANUFG ADDITL TANGIB REVNUE PROFIT ";
550   PRINT "INTANG  NET"
560   PRINT "             WE GET   COST   COST   COST           ";
570   PRINT " COST BENEFIT"
580   PRINT "======= ====== ====== ====== ====== ====== ====== == "
590   FOR K=1 TO 10
600   K1=1+3*(K-1)
610   K2=3*K
620   U=L[K]+C[K]
630   PRINT  USING 640;K,W$[K1,K2],L[K],C[K],U,Q[K],T[K],I[K],N[K]
640   IMAGE 5D,5X,3A,4X,7(4D,3X)
650   NEXT K
660   PRINT
670   PRINT "COMPETITIVE ADVANTAGE(MIN,MAX) :";Y1;Y2
680   PRINT
690   PRINT "INTER-OPTION CORRELATION";I1
700   PRINT
```

```
705    PRINT "NUMBER ØF ITERATIØNS ";NO
706    PRINT
710    RETURN
720    L[1]=M[1]
730    L[2]=0
740    L[3]=M[2]
750    L[4]=M[3]
760    L[5]=M[3]+M[4]
770    L[6]=M[5]
780    L[7]=M[3]+M[5]
790    L[8]=M[4]
800    L[9]=M[6]
810    L[10]=M[7]
820    Q[1]=P[1]
830    Q[2]=0
840    Q[3]=P[2]
850    Q[4]=P[3]
860    Q[5]=P[3]+P[4]
870    Q[6]=P[5]
880    Q[7]=P[3]+P[5]
890    Q[8]=P[4]
900    Q[9]=P[6]
910    Q[10]=P[7]
920    L1=1
930    FØR K=1 TØ 10
940    Q[K]=Q[K]*.114
950    L[K]=L[K]*.114
960    T[K]=Q[K]-L[K]-C[K]
970    N[K]=T[K]-I[K]
980    Z[K]=0
990    NEXT K
1000   RETURN
1010   FØR N1=1 TØ NO
1020   IF I1=0 THEN 1060
1030   GØSUB 5000
1040   X1=H1
1050   Y=((Y1+Y2)*.5+(Y2-Y1)*.25*H2)/100
1060   FØR Ø1=1 TØ 7
1070   IF I1=1 THEN 1110
1080   GØSUB 5000
1090   X1=H1
1100   Y=((Y1+Y2)*.5+(Y2-Y1)*.25*H2)/100
1110   X[Ø1]=(A[Ø1]+B[Ø1])*.5+(B[Ø1]-A[Ø1])*.25*X1
1120   X[Ø1]=X[Ø1]*(1+Y)
1130   NEXT Ø1
1140   A1=P[1] MIN X[1]
1150   B1=(P[2]+X[3]) MIN (P[3]+X[2])
1160   C1=(P[3]+P[4]+X[5]) MIN (P[5]+X[3]+X[4])
1170   D1=(P[3]+P[5]+X[4]) MIN (P[4]+X[3]+X[5])
1180   E1=(P[6]+X[7]) MIN (P[7]+X[6])
1190   V=(((A1 MIN B1) MIN C1) MIN D1) MIN E1
1200   K=0
1210   IF V=P[1] THEN 1420
1220   IF V=X[1] THEN 1410
1230   IF V=P[2]+X[3] THEN 1400
1240   IF V=P[3]+X[2] THEN 1390
1250   IF V=P[3]+P[4]+X[5] THEN 1380
1260   IF V=P[5]+X[3]+X[4] THEN 1370
1270   IF V=P[3]+P[5]+X[4] THEN 1360
1280   IF V=P[4]+X[3]+X[5] THEN 1350
1290   IF V=P[6]+X[7] THEN 1340
1300   IF V=P[7]+X[6] THEN 1330
1310   PRINT "ERRØR"
1320   GØTØ 9999
1330   K=K+1
1340   K=K+1
1350   K=K+1
1360   K=K+1
1370   K=K+1
1380   K=K+1
1390   K=K+1
1400   K=K+1
1410   K=K+1
1420   K=K+1
1430   Z[K]=Z[K]+1
1440   NEXT N1
1450   FØR K=1 TØ 10
1460   Z[K]=Z[K]/NO
1470   NEXT K
1600   Q1=Q2=0
1610   FØR K=1 TØ 10
1620   Q1=Q1+Z[K]*T[K]
1630   Q2=Q2+Z[K]*I[K]
1640   NEXT K
1650   PRINT
1660   PRINT "EXPECTED PRØFIT:";Q1
1670   PRINT "EXPECTED INTANG:";-Q2
1680   PRINT "EXP. NET BENEF.:";Q1-Q2
1690   PRINT
1700   PRINT "WANT PRØBABILITIES";
1710   INPUT Z$
1720   IF Z$[1,1]="N" THEN 1800
1730   PRINT
1740   PRINT "ØUTCØME PRØBABILITY"
1750   PRINT "======= ==========="
1760   FØR K=1 TØ 10
1770   PRINT USING 1780;K,Z[K]
1780   IMAGE 5D,7X,1D.3D
1790   NEXT K
1800   RETURN
```

```
4000  PRINT "CHANGE CODE:0=NO MORE,1=PRICE,2=COMP.BID,3=OP.CORR.,4=#ITER■
4010  PRINT
4020  PRINT "CHANGE ";
4030  INPUT Z2
4040  GOTO Z2 OF 4100,4200,4300,4400
4050  RETURN
4100  PRINT "INPUT OPTION #,NEW PRICE ";
4120  INPUT O1,P[O1]
4130  GOTO 4020
4200  PRINT "INPUT OPTION #,MIN,MAX ";
4210  INPUT O1,A[O1],B[O1]
4220  GOTO 4020
4300  PRINT "INPUT CORRELATION CHOICE ";
4310  INPUT I1
4312  IF I1=0 THEN 4020
4313  IF I1=1 THEN 4020
4314  PRINT "INTER-OPTION CORRELATION MUST BE 0 OR 1"
4315  GOTO 4300
4320  GOTO 4020
4400  PRINT "INPUT # OF ITERATIONS ";
4410  INPUT NO
4420  GOTO 4020
4990  REM INDEPENDENT NORMAL (0,1) RANDOM NUMBER SUBROUTINE
5000  J1=RND(0)
5010  J2=RND(0)
5020  P9=2*3.14159
5030  H1=SQR(-2*LOG(J1))*COS(P9*J2)
5040  H2=SQR(-2*LOG(J1))*SIN(P9*J2)
5050  RETURN
6000  DATA 6700,9400,6700,7610
6010  DATA 5500,5200,5500,6490
6020  DATA 900,1500,1200,1460
6030  DATA 3500,4700,2700,3920
6040  DATA 2700,3100,2500,2830
6050  DATA 4700,5500,3700,4830
6060  DATA 2300,2900,3000,4000
6100  DATA 126,0
6110  DATA 0,200
6120  DATA 115,0
6130  DATA 21,200
6140  DATA 70,50
6150  DATA 74,150
6160  DATA 91,200
6170  DATA 60,50
6180  DATA 94,0
6190  DATA 50,180
6200  DATA 0,0
6300  DATA 100
6400  DATA 1
8000  W$[1,30]="1    2  3  3+45  3+54  6  7  "
8010  V$[1,32]="ABCDEFGHABCDEFG........HABC....."
8020  V$[33,56]="...DEFG.ABCDE........FGH"
8030  RETURN
9999  END
```

CONCORN KITCHENS [15]

Mr. Conrad, Marketing Director of the Ethnic Foods Division of Concorn Kitchens was dissatisfied with the planning process used in his division. Previously, brand managers had prepared a document containing a review of past performance of each product and a pro forma profit and loss statement which implicitly contained a recommended price, and promotion and advertising strategy for the following year. It was viewed by most brand managers as a "commitment" for sales and profits that would be forthcoming from the product.

Mr. Conrad felt that these documents were "ploys" used by his subordinates to obtain as many marketing resources as possible. He felt that the plans often had no relation to historical performance and that no clear meaning could be assigned to the sales and profit numbers included in the plan. He was not sure if these numbers represented goals or predictions. It was never clear how the sales figures were related to the marketing inputs, nor what would be the consequences of certain resource allocations.

As an example, he cited the lack of relationship between the 1973 plan and actual performance, particularly for one of the company's products—Tacos. He noted that because sales did not develop as anticipated during the first part of the year he was forced to cut advertising budgets for subsequent quarters. He stated, "If the original projections had been better this would never have happened and we would not be in the profit squeeze we now face."

The Operations Research Manager, Mr. Kendall, suggested that the preparation of the marketing plan could be expedited by the development of some computer models. He recommended that he be authorized to develop such models. An Operations Research project was approved and undertaken, the results of which are summarized in the report shown in Exhibit 1, from Mr. Kendall.

Based on this report, Mr. Conrad decided to try the system out on two products—Matzo Balls & Tacos. The market research staff was requested to get together information necessary to use the models. The result of this effort is reported in Exhibit 2. Mr. Conrad now intends to try out the new system. The product history for tacos is given in Exhibit 3; for matzo balls in Exhibit 4.

The case presents a situation in which a computer based macro planning model was proposed as a way of doing strategic planning for two lines of grocery products. From a product point of view the case can be considered a life cycle problem where one product has matured while the other still has growth potential. The implications of this becomes clear as the model is used to "optimize" sales and profits. From a technical point of view the case raises issues concerning appropriate factors to consider in the planning process and how to represent these in a quantitative way. The model uses "response coefficients" to deal with the "best" strategy question. This raises the issue of sources of information (e.g.,—experiments, use of historical data, marketing information systems, etc.).

Exhibit 1

To: Mr. Conrad
From: Mr. Kendall
Subject: Computer Planning Model (PLAN)

We believe that a planning process should include the following steps.

1) Data on past performance should be stored in an easily accessible way and these data should form the basis of a first projection of future outcomes.

2) Projections of key components of the plan should be made assuming continuation of past trends and strategies. These component projections should then be combined into a pro forma profit and loss statement for each product. (We call this a *Planning Base*.)

3) Alternate plans should then be developed which explicitly take into account the relationships between changes in spending, prices and resulting levels of sales and profits. These alternate plans should be evaluated by comparison to the Planning Base.

---

[15] This case and the computer model were originally developed by Gerald J. Eskin, Lecturer in Marketing, Graduate School of Business, Stanford University. Revisions have been made by Peter Webb, doctoral candidate, and David B. Montgomery, Professor of Management, both of the Stanford Graduate School of Business.

These ideas have been incorporated into a timesharing computer model called PLAN (see page 61 for the program listing). It should be possible for your staff to use the model simply by following the steps shown on the sample output.

After you specify the product to be considered, the computer will retrieve and display information on the history of that product.

It will then make linear extrapolations of key components.[16] These extrapolations are purely mechanical in nature and will not always be considered appropriate. Provisions for overriding the projections have been made so that when you feel market, market share or costs can be better projected subjectively this can be done. In the case of costs, we have in general projected totals; but as you can see from the printout, storage space has been provided to consider cost as a function of sales, rather than fixed in total.

Given that these first projections are intended to show the results of continuing historical strategies, the override option should not be used to indicate new trends that might develop from a shift in strategy. Such effects are considered in the next stage of analysis.

The remainder of the program is designed to allow experimentation with alternate marketing plans in order to improve on the base projection. To use this section, the computer must know something about the responsiveness of sales to various marketing tools. This knowledge is summarized in the form of response coefficients to be supplied by the user. These are defined as:

$$\frac{\% \text{ change in sales}}{\% \text{ change in inputs}} \text{ (e.g., price, adv., etc.)}$$

The way in which these coefficients affect sales is illustrated in the following tables:

Change in Advertising (% change from Planning Base)	Percent change in Sales for an advertising response coefficient of:	
	.2	.4
+20%	+4%	+8%
+10%	+2%	+4%
Same Adv. as in Planning Base	Same Sales as PB	Same Sales as PB
−10%	−2%	−4%
−20%	−4%	−8%

Change in Price (as % of price in Planning Base)	Percent change in Sales for a price response coefficient of:	
	−1	−2
+10%	−10%	−20%
No change	No change	No change
−10%	+10%	+20%

Note that the price response coefficients should always be negative.

We realize that complete knowledge is not always available on response coefficients but believed that your years of marketing experience and past research efforts should allow rough estimates to be made. When you are unsure of the exact value you may wish to use the option at the end of the program which allows sensitivity testing through trying the same plan with different response coefficients.

---

[16] The extrapolation is done using both the average value of a variable during the past five years and a weighted combination of past trends. Specifically, the relation used to project i years ahead is:

$$\text{Projected Value in Year } i = \text{Average Value During Past 5 Years}$$
$$+ (.2+.1i) * \left\{ 2[\text{Value last year} - \text{Value 5 years ago}] \right.$$
$$\left. + [\text{Value 2 years ago} - \text{Value 4 years ago}] \right\}$$

This is equivalent to linear extrapolation based on a least squares fit to the five year history.

When attempting to test the sensitivity of response coefficients remember that the co-efficients are defined in terms of *changes* from the Planning Base, hence a sensitivity test can only be performed on a plan that is *different* from the base plan.[17]

The following technical notes are provided on the program:

A. *Units of Measure*

    (1)   Market and Sales are measured in thousands of cases (12 units to the case).

    (2)   All dollar values are to be entered in thousands and all resulting computer outputs are in thousands.

    (3)   Price is the case price charged by Concorn. Retail prices are roughly 30% higher.

B. *Accounting Conventions*

    (1)   Gross Contribution Margin = Price − Variable Production Cost

    (2)   Overhead includes only manufacturing expense (fixed production costs and depreciation). General and administrative expenses are not included in product level profit and loss statements at Concorn (sales force expense is considered G & A).

    (3)   Promotional includes expenditures on:

        (a) Trade allowances (temporary price reductions)
        (b) Cents-off packs and coupons
        (c) Point-of-sale material

C. *Other Program Conventions*

    (1)   Response coefficients are specified by inputting five numerical values, each separated by commas, to correspond to each of the five coming years. Remember to use a negative sign for the price coefficients. Since response coefficients measure the change from the planning base level, no change in the P/L will occur unless a new marketing variable level is specified.

    (2)   Sample output is attached. Below is a flow chart of the analysis.

---

[17]The computer model combines price, advertising, and promotion response functions in the following way:

New unit sales projection = base plan unit sales projection X RF,

$$\text{Where } RF = \left(\frac{\text{New Price}}{\text{Base Plan Price}}\right)^{PRC} * \left(\frac{\text{New Advertising Level}}{\text{Base Plan Advertising Level}}\right)^{ARC} *$$

$$\left(\frac{\text{New Promotion Level}}{\text{Base Plan Promotion Level}}\right)^{PRRC}$$

RF = Response Factor
PRC = Price Response Coefficient
ARC = Advertising Response Coefficient
PRRC = Promotion Response Coefficient

Response coefficients can be thought of as elasticities in economic terms. That is, they represent percentage changes of projected unit sales relative to base plan sales when price, advertising, and/or promotion are changed relative to their base plan levels.

PLAN Flowchart

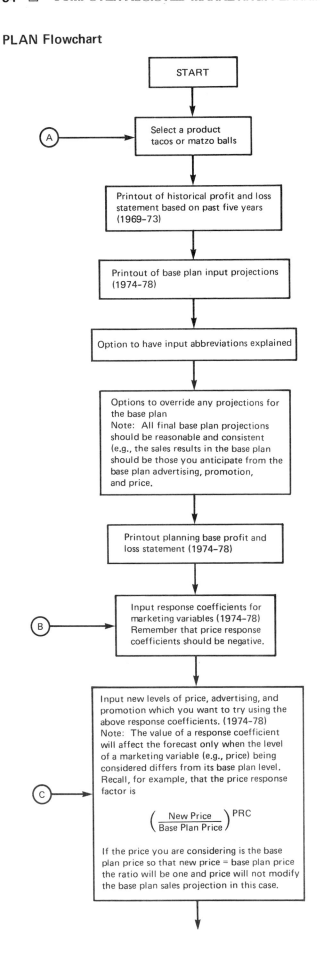

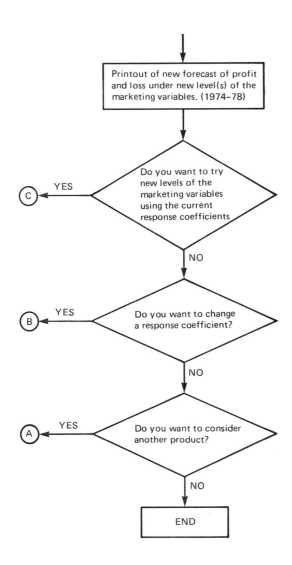

PLAN Sample Run

TEST

HISTØRICAL FILE

	1969	1970	1971	1972	1973
MARKET	1000	2000	3000	4000	5000
SHARE	0.200	0.200	0.200	0.200	0.200
PRICE	2.500	2.500	2.250	2.250	2.250
GRØSS C MARG	1.000	1.000	0.800	0.800	0.800
SALES VØL	200	400	600	800	1000
SALES $	500	1000	1350	1800	2250
GR C MARG	200	400	480	640	800
ØVERHEAD	100	100	100	150	150
GR MARGIN	100	300	380	490	650
ADVERT.	20	20	20	20	20
PRØMØTIØN	30	30	30	30	30
NET ØP PR	50	250	330	440	600

BASE PLAN INPUT PRØJECTIØNS

	LINE #	1974	1975	1976	1977	1978
MARKET	1	6000	7000	8000	9000	10000
SHARE	2	0.200	0.200	0.200	0.200	0.200
PRICE	3	2.125	2.050	1.975	1.900	1.825
GR C MG	4	0.700	0.640	0.580	0.520	0.460
ØVHD/UN	5	0.000	0.000	0.000	0.000	0.000
ØV CØNS	6	165	180	195	210	225
ADV/UN	7	0.000	0.000	0.000	0.000	0.000
AD CST	8	20	20	20	20	20
PRØM/UN	9	0.000	0.000	0.000	0.000	0.000
PRØM CT	10	30	30	30	30	30

```
DO YOU WANT AN EXPLANATION OF THE INPUTS?(0=NO,1=YES)
? 1


'MARKET' IS TOTAL INDUSTRY MARKET
'SHARE' IS CONCORN'S SHARE OF THE TOTAL INDUSTRY MARKET
'GR C MG' IS GROSS CONTRIBUTION MARGIN
'OVHD/UN' IS OVERHEAD PER UNIT (VARIABLE OVERHEAD COST)
'OV/CONS' IS OVERHEAD CONSTANT (FIXED OVERHEAD COST)
'ADV/UN' IS ADVERTISING PER UNIT
'AD CST' IS ADVERTISING CONSTANT
'PROM/UN' IS PROMOTION PER UNIT
'PROM CT' IS PROMOTION CONSTANT
'NET OP PR' IS NET OPERATING PROFIT

DO YOU WISH TO OVERRIDE ANY PROJECTIONS?(0=NO,1=YES)
? 1
WHICH LINE?3
NEW VALUES?2.25,2.25,2.25,2.25,2.25

ANY OTHERS?(0=NO,1=YES)
? 1


WHICH LINE?4
NEW VALUES?.8,.8,.8,.8,.8

ANY OTHERS?(0=NO,1=YES)
? 1

WHICH LINE?6
NEW VALUES?150,200,200,200,250

ANY OTHERS?(0=NO,1=YES)
? 0


PLANNING BASE P/L
                1974    1975    1976    1977    1978

SALES VOL       1200    1400    1600    1800    2000
SALES $         2700    3150    3600    4050    4500
GR C MARG        960    1120    1280    1440    1600
OVERHEAD         150     200     200     200     250
GR MARGIN        810     920    1030    1240    1350
ADVERT.           20      20      20      20      20
PROMOTION         30      30      30      30      30
NET OP PR        760     870    1030    1190    1300

SPECIFY RESPONSE COEF TO BE USED FOR EACH OF 5 YRS

PRICE           ?-2,-2,-2,-2,-2
ADVERTISING     ?.2,.2,.2,.2,.2
PROMOTION       ?.4,.4,.4,.4,.4

WHICH MARKETING VARIABLE DO YOU WANT TO CHANGE
PRICE=1,ADVERTISING=2,PROMOTION=3
? 2
SPECIFY NEW LEVELS BY YEAR?30,40,50,60,70

ANY OTHERS?(0=NO,1=YES)
? 0


                1974    1975    1976    1977    1978

SALES VOL       1301    1608    1922    2242    2569
SALES $         2928    3618    4324    5045    5781
GR C MARG       1041    1287    1537    1794    2056
OVERHEAD         150     200     200     200     250
GR MARGIN        891    1087    1337    1594    1806
ADVERT.           30      40      50      60      70
PROMOTION         30      30      30      30      30
NET OP PR        831    1017    1257    1504    1706

DO YOU WISH TO TRY ANOTHER PLAN?(0=NO,1=YES)
? 0

DO YOU WISH TO CHANGE A RESPONSE COEFFICIENT?(0=NO,1=YES)
? 0

DO YOU WISH TO CONSIDER ANOTHER PRODUCT?(0=NO,1=YES)
? 0

DONE
```

Exhibit 2

Memo to: Mr. Conrad

From: Marketing Research Staff

Subject: Data for PLAN Computer Model

Per Mr. Kendall's request we have provided historical data on Matzo Balls and Tacos for inclusion in the computer data base. This information will be updated as new data becomes available.

With respect to the request for detailed variable production cost data, it is estimated that raw materials costs will increase at a rate of 7% per year over the next 5 years (1974–1978) for tacos, and 5% for matzo balls. It is further estimated that net labor costs (direct labor cost adjusted for change in productivity) will remain constant over the same period. Materials (including packaging) and labor share equally in direct production costs.

Current indications suggest inflation will be a serious problem over the next five years. This means that not only may production and overhead costs be higher than projected, but also promotion and advertising dollars may buy less. It is therefore suggested that to the extent inflation is considered a problem, planning base P/L projections should be re-evaluated accordingly.

The request for response coefficient information is more difficult to satisfy. A controlled experiment was conducted on Tacos two years ago which provides some information on this product. The results of that test were:

price coef.	−1.6 (sig. at 5% level)
adv. coef.	.1 (not significant)

We suspect that over time the price elasticity coefficient is rising (larger negative values) while the adv. coefficient is falling although we cannot prove this assertion.

There are no data available on Matzo Balls, but we do have some estimates on some other products which may have similar values to those of Matzo Balls in that they are also new convenience foods in our line. They are:

	Price Coef.	Adv.
Pizza Popups	−1.2	.3
Egg Rolls	−1.4	.4

Exhibit 3
TACOS' Product History

The Taco Mix market started in the mid-1950's as a commercialization of some processing methods that were developed as part of World War II technology. Concorn was one of the first national brands in the market and, for a number of years, was the leading brand.

As the market grew, several other major companies entered the market. These companies had the advantage of having major sources of revenue in other higher margin industries plus experience in technologies important to the Taco Mix market.

By 1969, the market had slowed and Concorn was tied for second place with Julia Child at about 20% of the market. Gambles Deluxe had become the leading brand with 27% of the market following many years during which they dominated the market in terms of spending, primarily on advertising (behind the slogan "I'll take a Gamble").

During the past five years, sales promotion had become an increasingly important marketing tool. In 1973, 90% of Concorn's volume moved at a dealing rate of $1 per case in order to hold distribution. Little was passed on to the consumer. It was probable that the promotion elasticity coefficient was not the same for promotion increases and promotion decreases. It was felt that further promotional allowances would have little impact, unless they were greater than 20–30%. However, it was likely that the market would respond sharply to promotion decreases.

Consumer promotions are considered generally ineffective as they are invariably matched by competition. There are no clear data about whether as high a percentage of competitor tonnage moves under a deal.

There is some indication that Concorn technology has not kept pace with the industry and Concorn may have a marginal product disadvantage.

Tacos used about 35% of the output of a $40 million plant (about 2/3 equipment, 1/3 building). The plant, currently operating at 90% capacity, did not produce matzo balls. Depreciation life was 10 years on equipment and 20 years on building, both building and equipment were fully depreciated.[18] The building was adequate but the equipment somewhat obsolete. As a result, it was projected that Concorn would suffer a 10% cost disadvantage relative to the market leader over the next five years (this figure drops to 5% for the company second in the market, and zero beyond that).

A recent study to determine the profitability of replacing obsolete equipment indicated the cost (150% of initial cost of current equipment) would be prohibitive.

If taco demand fell, other products would not be likely to use new excess capacity.

In 1973, tacos used 8% of a $9,000,000 divisional sales force operation. This expense was not included in computing net operating profit. (As noted earlier, sales force expense is considered part of general administrative expenses which are not included in product level P/L statements at Concorn.) Sales force expense at current operating levels was expected to increase 2–3% per year.

Ingredient costs have been rising, causing a deterioration in our margin. In the past Concorn felt that these rising costs could not be passed on to the consumer given the highly competitive nature of the market.

While ad tests showed Concorn advertising to be of equal quality to competition and perhaps marginally superior, awareness studies showed the leading brand to be getting credit with consumers for the principal product benefits claimed by Concorn.

The following are the 1973 share of market and media expenditure data:

	Share	Media $ Million
Concorn	16%	1.5
Gambles Deluxe	30%	3.5
Julia Child	20%	2.5
Private Label	25%	—
All Others	9%	—

---

[18] By 1969, all taco equipment was fully depreciated. The building, however, was not fully depreciated until 1973, hence depreciation expense on the building (straight line) appears in the overhead account of the historical file. Since the computer forecast of overhead is based on these historical data and these expenses will not all continue, the mechanical forecast will overestimate overhead by $233.

Plan vs. Actual	1973	
	Plan (000)	Actual (000)
Market	41000	40800
Share	.17	.157
Sales Volume	6970	6406
Sales $	36592	33629
price 5.25 case (.55 per pkg. retail)		
Gross Cont. Margin	12615	11466
unit	(1.81)	(1.79)
Overhead	2000	2000
Gross Margin	10615	9466
Advertising	2000	1500
Promotion	5500	5783
Net Operating Profit	3115	2183

PLAN Sample Run for Tacos

```
WHICH PRODUCT DO YOU WANT TO CONSIDER?(0=TACOS,1=MATZO BALLS)
? 0

TACOS


HISTORICAL FILE
                1969      1970      1971      1972      1973

MARKET         39000     40000     40600     40800     40800
SHARE          0.192     0.185     0.160     0.165     0.157
PRICE          5.250     5.250     5.250     5.250     5.250
GROSS C MARG   1.900     1.870     1.840     1.810     1.790

SALES VOL       7488      7400      6496      6732      6406
SALES $        39312     38850     34104     35343     33629
GR C MARG      14227     13838     11953     12185     11466
OVERHEAD        2160      2100      2050      2020      2000
GR MARGIN      12067     11738      9903     10165      9466
ADVERT.         2114      2105      1561      1610      1500
PROMOTION       5028      5032      5101      5500      5783
NET OP PR       4925      4601      3241      3055      2183


BASE PLAN INPUT PROJECTIONS
          LINE #   1974      1975      1976      1977      1978

MARKET       1    41560     42000     42440     42880     43320
SHARE        2    0.145     0.136     0.127     0.118     0.109
PRICE        3    5.250     5.250     5.250     5.250     5.250
GR C MG      4    1.758     1.730     1.702     1.674     1.646
OVHD/UN      5    0.000     0.000     0.000     0.000     0.000
OV CONS      6     1946      1906      1866      1826      1786
ADV/UN       7    0.000     0.000     0.000     0.000     0.000
AD CST       8     1261      1089       916       744       572
PROM/UN      9    0.000     0.000     0.000     0.000     0.000
PROM CT     10     5882      6080      6278      6476      6673

DO YOU WANT AN EXPLANATION OF THE INPUTS?(0=NO,1=YES)
? 0

DO YOU WISH TO OVERRIDE ANY PROJECTIONS?(0=NO,1=YES)
? 0


PLANNING BASE P/L
                1974      1975      1976      1977      1978

SALES VOL       6018      5704      5381      5051      4713
SALES $        31594     29944     28252     26519     24744
GR C MARG      10579      9867      9159      8456      7758
OVERHEAD        1946      1906      1866      1826      1786
GR MARGIN       8633      7961      7293      6630      5972
ADVERT.         1261      1089       917       744       572
PROMOTION       5882      6080      6278      6476      6673
NET OP PR       1490       792        99      -590     -1273
```

Exhibit 4
Matzo Balls' Product History

Concorn entered the matzo ball market in 1968, correctly anticipating the growth trend in that segment of the ethnic foods market. At that time, the major competitors in the market were the first national brand—Paulicci's Best with 40%—Zede's Matzo Balls with 20%, and a number of local or regional brands concentrated in such major metropolitan areas as New York, Miami Beach, Los Angeles, Chicago, and Philadelphia.

By 1971, the growth trend in the market and the attractive margins had led the major chains to introduce private label (store brand) matzo balls with strong local advertising and shelf space support. Paulicci's Best initiated a price cut, which the other brands followed, in an effort to reduce the price spread between the advertised and private label brands.

In addition, each brand reacted to the 1971 market situation in different ways. Paulicci's Best de-emphasized sales promotion, and increased its advertising behind Stan Freeburger's "Have a Ball" commercials. Zede's held to its historical pattern of promotion and advertising spending, but put its money behind the introduction of new, improved king-sized matzo balls. Concorn's response to the situation is reflected in the historical file—a strong emphasis on sales promotion and sales execution efforts to get in-store trade support. Response to promotional efforts is less well known for matzo balls than for tacos, due to the shorter product history and position in the product life cycle.

Matzo balls used about 75% of the output of an $8 million plant (about 2/3 equipment, 1/3 building). The plant was operating at 90% capacity. Depreciation life was 10 years on equipment and 20 years on building. Depreciation expense (straight line) was included in the overhead account.

In 1973, matzo balls used 3% of the divisional sales force operation. As with tacos, this expense wqs not included in computing net operating profit.

The following are the 1973 share of market and media expenditure data:

	Share	Media $ Million
Concorn	10.0%	2.0
Paulicci's	42.5%	7.5
Zede's	18.0%	4.0
Private Label	21.0%	—
All Others	8.5%	—

Product quality and advertising claims are effectively equal for all brands.

	1973	
Plan vs. Actual	Plan (000)	Actual (000)
Market	36500	36500
Share	.105	.10
Sales Volume	3832	3650
Sales $	15711	14965
price 4.10 case (.49 retail)		
Gross Cont. Margin	8430	8030
unit	(2.20)	(2.20)
Overhead	1500	1540
Gross Margin	6930	6490
Advertising	2000	2000
Promotion	3400	3600
Net Operating Profit	1530	890

PLAN Sample Run For Matzo Balls

```
WHICH PRODUCT DO YOU WANT TO CONSIDER?(0=TACOS,1=MATZO BALLS)
? 1

MATZO BALLS

HISTORICAL FILE
              1969    1970    1971    1972    1973

MARKET       21000   24500   28900   32700   36500
SHARE        0.090   0.105   0.105   0.100   0.100
PRICE        4.600   4.600   4.100   4.100   4.100
GROSS C MARG 2.600   2.600   2.200   2.200   2.200
```

Discussion Assignment
Concorn Kitchens

1. For either *tacos or matzo balls*:

    a. Analyze the products' historical position.

    b. What are the constraints on management action?

    c. Develop a defensible base plan.

    d. What range of response coefficients appear reasonable? Why?

    e. Use the PLAN program to help develop a product strategy for 1974–78. This should involve both an investigation of alternative and sensitivity analysis of assumptions.

    Be prepared to defend your assumptions, alternatives considered, and final product strategy selected.

2. Do you feel the Concorn planning system is a useful one? What changes or improvements would you like to see in the computer program?

SALES VOL	1890	2573	3035	3270	3650
SALES $	8694	11834	12441	13407	14965
GR C MARG	4914	6689	6676	7194	8030
OVERHEAD	1440	1430	1510	1530	1540
GR MARGIN	3474	5209	5166	5664	6490
ADVERT.	2000	2000	2000	2000	2000
PROMOTION	1420	1700	3030	3200	3600
NET OP PR	54	1509	136	464	890

BASE PLAN INPUT PROJECTIONS

	LINE #	1974	1975	1976	1977	1978
MARKET	1	40480	44400	48320	52240	56160
SHARE	2	0.104	0.106	0.107	0.109	0.110
PRICE	3	3.850	3.700	3.550	3.400	3.250
GR C MG	4	2.000	1.880	1.760	1.640	1.520
OVHD/UN	5	0.000	0.000	0.000	0.000	0.000
OV CONS	6	1575	1600	1625	1650	1675
ADV/UN	7	0.000	0.000	0.000	0.000	0.000
AD CST	8	2000	2000	2000	2000	2000
PROM/UN	9	0.000	0.000	0.000	0.000	0.000
PROM CT	10	4348	4934	5520	6106	6692

```
DO YOU WANT AN EXPLANATION OF THE INPUTS?(0=NO,1=YES)
?0

DO YOU WISH TO OVERRIDE ANY PROJECTIONS?(0=NO,1=YES)
?0
```

PLANNING BASE P/L

	1974	1975	1976	1977	1978
SALES VOL	4230	4706	5194	5694	6206
SALES $	16286	17414	18440	19360	20168
GR C MARG	8460	8848	9142	9338	9433
OVERHEAD	1575	1600	1625	1650	1675
GR MARGIN	6885	7248	7517	7688	7758
ADVERT.	2000	2000	2000	2000	2000
PROMOTION	4348	4934	5520	6106	6692
NET OP PR	537	314	-3	-418	-934

PLAN PROGRAM LISTING

```
1    REM   PLAN BRAND MARKETING MIX PLANNING MODEL 7/23/73
2    REM   DATA SEQUENCE IN DATA STATEMENTS IS "NAME", AND THEN
3    REM   FOR EACH OF THE PAST FIVE YEARS: TOTAL MARKET, MARKET
4    REM   SHARE, PRICE, GROSS C MARG, OVERHEAD, ADV., PROMOTION
5    IMAGE 13A,8D,8D,8D,8D,8D
6    IMAGE 13A,4D.3D,4D.3D,4D.3D,4D.3D,4D.3D
8    IMAGE 13A,3D,8D,8D,8D,8D,8D
9    IMAGE 13A,3D,4D.3D,4D.3D,4D.3D,4D.3D,4D.3D
10   DIM A[4,5],H[10,5],S[8,5],T[5],V[12,5],W[4,5],Z[5],J$[72],K$[70]
11   DIM D$[2],E$[3],F$[5],G$[11],H$[9],I$[12]
12   DIM A$[5],B$[11],M[10,5]
13   DIM O$[25]
14   LET N=0
15   READ D$,E$,F$,G$,H$
20   DATA "NO","YES","PRICE","ADVERTISING","PROMOTION"
25   FOR I=1 TO 8
30   READ J$[(I-1)*9+1,I*9]
35   NEXT I
40   DATA "SALES VOL","SALES $  ","GR C MARG","OVERHEAD"
45   DATA "GR MARGIN","ADVERT.  ","PROMOTION","NET OP PR"
50   FOR I=1 TO 10
55   READ K$[(I-1)*7+1,I*7]
60   NEXT I
65   DATA "MARKET ","SHARE  ","PRICE  ","GR C MG"
70   DATA "OVHD/UN","OV CONS","ADV/UN "
75   DATA "AD CST ","PROM/UN","PROM CT"
76   READ A$
77   PRINT
78   PRINT "WHICH PRODUCT DO YOU WANT TO CONSIDER?";
79   PRINT "(0=TACOS,1=MATZO BALLS)"
81   INPUT B1
82   IF B1=1 THEN 87
83   PRINT
84   PRINT A$
85   PRINT
86   GOTO 95
87   FOR I=1 TO 7
88   FOR J=1 TO 5
89   READ M[I,J]
90   NEXT J
91   NEXT I
92   READ B$
93   PRINT
94   PRINT B$
95   PRINT
96   FOR I=1 TO 7
97   FOR J=1 TO 5
98   READ H[I,J]
100  NEXT J
105  NEXT I
107  RESTORE
```

```
110  FØR J=1 TØ 5
115  LET S[1,J]=H[1,J]*H[2,J]
120  LET S[2,J]=S[1,J]*H[3,J]
125  LET S[3,J]=S[1,J]*H[4,J]
130  LET S[4,J]=H[5,J]
135  LET S[5,J]=S[3,J]-S[4,J]
140  LET S[6,J]=H[6,J]
145  LET S[7,J]=H[7,J]
150  LET S[8,J]=S[5,J]-S[6,J]-S[7,J]
155  NEXT J
174  PRINT
175  PRINT "HISTØRICAL FILE"
176  LET @S=" "
180  PRINT  USING 5;@S,1969,1970,1971,1972,1973
185  PRINT
186  LET @S="MARKET"
190  PRINT  USING 5;Q$,H[1,1],H[1,2],H[1,3],H[1,4],H[1,5]
191  LET ?S="SHARE"
195  PRINT  USING 6;Q$,H[2,1],H[2,2],H[2,3],H[2,4],H[2,5]
196  LET Q$="PRICE"
200  PRINT  USING 6;Q$,H[3,1],H[3,2],H[3,3],H[3,4],H[3,5]
201  LET Q$="GRØSS C MARG"
205  PRINT  USING 6;Q$,H[4,1],H[4,2],H[4,3],H[4,4],H[4,5]
210  PRINT
215  GØSUB 935
220  FØR J=1 TØ 5
225  LET H[8,J]=H[6,J]
230  LET H[6,J]=H[5,J]
235  LET H[10,J]=H[7,J]
240  LET H[5,J]=H[7,J]=H[9,J]=0
245  NEXT J
250  FØR X=1 TØ 10
255  LET R=0
260  FØR Y=1 TØ 5
265  LET R=R+H[X,Y]
270  NEXT Y
275  FØR Y=1 TØ 5
280  LET V[X,Y]=.2*R+.1*(Y+2)*(-2*H[X,1]-H[X,2]+H[X,4]+2*H[X,5])
285  NEXT Y
290  NEXT X
295  PRINT
300  PRINT "BASE PLAN INPUT PRØJECTIØNS"
305  PRINT "           LINE #   1974     1975     1976     1977     1978"
310  PRINT
315  FØR I=1 TØ 10
320  FØR J=1 TØ 5
325  LET Z[J]=INT(1000*V[I,J]+.5)/1000
330  NEXT J
335  GØTØ I ØF 340,350,350,350,350,340,350,340,350,340
340  PRINT  USING 8;K$[(I-1)*7+1,I*7],I,Z[1],Z[2],Z[3],Z[4],Z[5]
345  GØTØ 355
350  PRINT  USING 9;K$[(I-1)*7+1,I*7],I,Z[1],Z[2],Z[3],Z[4],Z[5]
355  NEXT I
356  PRINT
357  PRINT "DØ YØU WANT AN EXPLANATIØN ØF THE INPUTS?(0=NØ,1=YES)"
359  INPUT B2
360  IF B2=0 THEN 372
361  PRINT
362  PRINT "'MARKET' IS TØTAL INDUSTRY MARKET"
363  PRINT "'SHARE' IS CØNCØRN'S SHARE ØF THE TØTAL INDUSTRY MARKET"
364  PRINT "'GR C MG' IS GRØSS CØNTRIBUTIØN MARGIN"
365  PRINT "'ØVHD/UN' IS ØVERHEAD PER UNIT (VARIABLE ØVERHEAD CØST)"
366  PRINT "'ØV/CØNS' IS ØVERHEAD CØNSTANT (FIXED ØVERHEAD CØST)"
367  PRINT "'ADV/UN' IS ADVERTISING PER UNIT"
368  PRINT "'AD CST' IS ADVERTISING CØNSTANT"
369  PRINT "'PRØM/UN' IS PRØMØTIØN PER UNIT"
370  PRINT "'PRØM CT' IS PRØMØTIØN CØNSTANT"
371  PRINT "'NET ØP PR' IS NET ØPERATING PRØFIT"
372  PRINT
373  PRINT "DØ YØU WISH TØ ØVERRIDE ANY PRØJECTIØNS?(0=NØ,1=YES)'
374  INPUT B3
375  IF B3=0 THEN 430
380  PRINT "WHICH LINE";
385  INPUT Y
390  PRINT "NEW VALUES";
395  INPUT V[Y,1],V[Y,2],V[Y,3],V[Y,4],V[Y,5]
400  PRINT
405  PRINT "ANY ØTHERS?(0=NØ,1=YES)"
410  INPUT B4
415  PRINT
420  IF B4=0 THEN 430
425  GØTØ 380
430  FØR Y=1 TØ 5
435  LET W[1,Y]=V[3,Y]
440  NEXT Y
445  GØSUB 860
450  PRINT
455  PRINT
460  LET N=1
465  PRINT "PLANNING BASE P/L"
470  GØSUB 925
475  FØR X=1 TØ 5
480  LET T[X]=S[1,X]
485  FØR Y=2 TØ 3
490  LET W[Y,X]=S[Y+4,X]
495  LET V[Y+9,X]=W[Y,X]
500  NEXT Y
505  LET V[7,X]=V[9,X]=0
510  LET V[8,X]=W[2,X]
515  LET V[10,X]=W[3,X]
```

```
520  NEXT X
525  PRINT "SPECIFY RESPØNSE CØEF TØ BE USED FØR EACH ØF 5 YRS"
530  PRINT
535  PRINT F$,
540  INPUT A[1,1],A[1,2],A[1,3],A[1,4],A[1,5]
545  PRINT G$,
550  INPUT A[2,1],A[2,2],A[2,3],A[2,4],A[2,5]
555  PRINT H$,
560  INPUT A[3,1],A[3,2],A[3,3],A[3,4],A[3,5]
575  PRINT
580  PRINT "WHICH MARKETING VARIABLE DØ YØU WANT TØ CHANGE"
581  PRINT "PRICE=1,ADVERTISING=2,PRØMØTIØN=3"
585  GØSUB 630
590  PRINT "SPECIFY NEW LEVELS BY YEAR";
595  INPUT W[Y,1],W[Y,2],W[Y,3],W[Y,4],W[Y,5]
600  PRINT
605  PRINT "ANY ØTHERS?(0=NØ,1=YES)"
610  INPUT B9
615  PRINT
620  IF B9=0 THEN 690
625  GØTØ 580
630  INPUT B9
635  LET Y=1
640  IF B9 <> 1 THEN 650
645  RETURN
650  LET Y=2
655  IF B9=2 THEN 645
660  LET Y=3
665  IF B9=3 THEN 645
670  LET Y=4
675  IF B9=4 THEN 645
680  PRINT "BAD FØRMAT RETYPE IT",
685  GØTØ 630
690  FØR X=1 TØ 5
695  LET R[X]=1
700  LET R[X]=R[X]*(W[1,X]/V[3,X])+A[1,X]
705  LET R[X]=R[X]*(W[2,X]/V[11,X])+A[2,X]
710  LET R[X]=R[X]*(W[3,X]/V[12,X])+A[3,X]
715  NEXT X
725  FØR X=1 TØ 5
730  LET S[1,X]=T[X]*R[X]
735  NEXT X
740  FØR X=1 TØ 5
745  LET V[8,X]=W[2,X]
750  LET V[10,X]=W[3,X]
755  NEXT X
760  GØSUB 860
765  GØSUB 920
770  PRINT "DØ YØU WISH TØ TRY ANØTHER PLAN?";
771  PRINT "(0=NØ,1=YES)"
775  INPUT B5
780  PRINT
785  IF B5=1 THEN 580
790  PRINT "DØ YØU WISH TØ CHANGE A RESPØNSE CØEFFICIENT?";
791  PRINT "(0=NØ,1=YES)"
795  INPUT B6
800  PRINT
805  IF B6=0 THEN 976
810  PRINT "WHICH ØNE?"
811  PRINT "(1=PRICE,2=ADVERTISING,3=PRØMØTIØN)"
815  GØSUB 630
820  PRINT "NEW VALUES";
825  INPUT A[Y,1],A[Y,2],A[Y,3],A[Y,4],A[Y,5]
830  PRINT
835  PRINT "ANY ØTHERS?(0=NØ,1=YES)"
840  INPUT B7
845  IF B7=1 THEN 810
855  GØTØ 690
860  FØR X=1 TØ 5
865  IF N <> 0 THEN 875
870  LET S[1,X]=V[1,X]*V[2,X]
875  LET S[2,X]=S[1,X]*W[1,X]
880  LET S[3,X]=S[1,X]*(V[4,X]+W[1,X]-V[3,X])
885  LET S[4,X]=S[1,X]*V[5,X]+V[6,X]
890  LET S[5,X]=S[3,X]-S[4,X]
895  LET S[6,X]=S[1,X]*V[7,X]+V[8,X]
900  LET S[7,X]=S[1,X]*V[9,X]+V[10,X]
905  LET S[8,X]=S[5,X]-S[6,X]-S[7,X]
910  NEXT X
915  RETURN
920  PRINT
925  LET Ø$=" "
926  PRINT  USING 5;Ø$,1974,1975,1976,1977,1978
930  PRINT
935  FØR I=1 TØ 8
940  FØR J=1 TØ 5
945  LET Z[J]=INT(S[I,J]+.5)
950  NEXT J
955  PRINT  USING 5;J$[(I-1)*9+1,I*9],Z[1],Z[2],Z[3],Z[4],Z[5]
960  NEXT I
962  PRINT
975  RETURN
976  PRINT "DØ YØU WISH TØ CØNSIDER ANØTHER PRØDUCT?";
977  PRINT "(0=NØ,1=YES)"
980  INPUT B8
982  IF B8=1 THEN 14
984  GØTØ 9999
1000 DATA "TACØS"
1001 DATA 39000.,40000.,40600.,40800.,40800.
```

```
1002    DATA .192,.185,.16,.165,.157
1003    DATA 5.25,5.25,5.25,5.25,5.25
1004    DATA 1.9,1.87,1.84,1.81,1.79
1005    DATA 2160,2100,2050,2020,2000
1006    DATA 2114,2105,1561,1610,1500
1007    DATA 5028,5032,5101,5500,5783
1010    DATA "MATZ0 BALLS"
1011    DATA 21000,24500,28900,32700,36500.
1012    DATA .09,.105,.105,.1,.1
1013    DATA 4.6,4.6,4.1,4.1,4.1
1014    DATA 2.6,2.6,2.2,2.2,2.2
1015    DATA 1440,1480,1510,1530,1540
1016    DATA 2000,2000,2000,2000,2000
1017    DATA 1420,1700,3030,3200,3600
9999    END
```

GENERAL FOODS CORPORATION-MAXIM [19]

In 1963 the Maxwell House Division of General Foods was the leading company in both the regular and soluble coffee markets. This dominant position was traceable to the company's historic strength in the regular coffee market, and the early development and introduction of high quality soluble (instant) coffees in the early 1950's. As a result of this flavor improvement in soluble coffee, category sales grew dramatically during the middle and late 1950's and were the leading growth factor in the total coffee market of that period.

Not content with this success, General Foods was aggressively developing another new coffee, produced by a process called freeze drying. This coffee was markedly different (in appearance and flavor) from either regular or "traditional" soluble coffees. The overriding problem during the initial development period was the high per unit production cost. By late 1962 the research group assigned to the problem expressed confidence that a freeze-dried coffee could be produced at a "reasonable" cost. Their recommendation to proceed was followed shortly by the assignment of a new product marketing group to the task of compiling appropriate consumer research and developing the most effective marketing positioning and strategy for the new brand. During 1963 this new product group, headed by Mr. Ken Carter,[20] who served as the Product Manager, worked towards the goal of preparing a fully defined national marketing plan by February of 1964. This national plan was designed to satisfy three needs:

1. Define the new product's positioning and potential share of market impact, as well as its ability to meet the company's financial guidelines for new entries.

2. Serve as the basis for a decision to either: proceed immediately to the national introduction stage, test market, or stop the development process.

3. Assuming a favorable decision to proceed with test and/or national market introduction, guide the implementation of these stages. (The marketing plan for a test market or regional introduction would be a scaled down version of the national plan.)

As the deadline for the completion of the marketing plan drew near, the problem of selecting the best "mix" from many alternatives of: *market positioning, pricing strategy, promotion and advertising budgets*, became acute.

In defining the optimum market positioning for the new product, three broad potential market positions became apparent:

1. A totally new kind of coffee
2. The best of the soluble category
3. As good as ground coffee with the convenience of soluble

Another vital consideration in properly positioning the new entry was the selection of a name for the brand. Should it be:

1. Maxwell House Freeze-Dried Coffee?
2. Freeze-Dried Instant Maxwell House?
3. A name with no Maxwell House connotations?

General Foods must develop a marketing plan for a new product—freeze dried coffee. Based on an extensive set of data on consumer and product research, decisions on product positioning, advertising, price, promotion, etc. must be made. Alternatively General Foods can decide to stop development of the project if it does not appear to be sufficiently profitable.

[19]This case was written by Professor George S. Day, Graduate School of Business, Stanford University.

[20]A disguised name used here to represent the several product executives who eventually worked on the project.

The basic issue involved was the desire to capitalize on the strength of the Maxwell House name and consumer acceptance at minimum cannibalization risk to other Maxwell House brands.

Each of the possible positions would require a different marketing approach. Each would also have its own impact on the final share of market goal identified in the marketing plan. Each would have to be evaluated in estimating the long run financial benefits to be gained by the introduction of the new freeze-dried entry. The determination of the most effective market positioning would also have direct effects on the selection of pricing strategy, promotion and budgets used to promote the brand.

The critical task of evaluating all viable alternatives involved and developing the best possible combination—to be detailed in the national marketing plan—was the assignment which Mr. Carter and the men of his Product Group faced in the closing months of 1963.

THE GENERAL FOODS CORPORATION

General Foods grew to its 1964 level of $1,338,000,000 in sales (see Exhibit 1)[21] through a series of mergers and consolidations that had begun in 1926 and that had gradually built up a corporate structure containing over sixty plants divided into six major domestic divisions: Maxwell House, Post, Jell-O, Birds-Eye, Kool-Aid and Institutional Food Service. Each division functioned as a highly autonomous unit. These divisions turned out a wide array of food products, including Maxwell House, Yuban and Sanka Coffees; Kool-Aid, Birds-Eye Frozen Foods; Post Cereals; Jell-O Desserts; Gaines Dog Foods; Minute Rice and many more.

Maxwell House Division. The organizational structure of the Maxwell House Division reflected its marketing orientation (see Exhibit 2). The Division believed that the size, complexity and competitive nature of the coffee business created the need for the "Business within a business" arrangement of product management. Key to the success of this system was having a small group of managers—such as Ken Carter—literally "run their own business" under general philosophy and strategy guidelines administered by Division's top management. In short, subject to the approval of management, Maxwell House Division Product Managers exercised the functional responsibility and authority of a "General Manager" of a given brand. This "General Manager" responsibility required that the Product Manager initiate the development of an integrated overall plan for marketing his brand, *secure* management's concurrence with this plan and *follow through* to ensure that each element of the plan was successfully and efficiently executed.

To discharge this "General Manager" responsibility to his brand, the Product Manager had to secure management concurrence on these primary objectives: (1) The competitive position the brand expects to occupy in the marketplace, (2) The brand's profit and volume objectives, (3) The advertising, promotion and pricing strategy and execution, (4) All auxiliary plans and operations necessary to realize these profit and sales objectives—including appropriate marketing research plans, product development plans, marketing tests, etc.

New Projects Evaluation Policy. An important consideration in the development of the new freeze-dried product's marketing position, objectives and strategies, was the financial requirement specified in General Foods' corporate policy for new entries. General Foods required each division to submit rate-of-return estimates for any project involving incremental outlays of more

---

[21]Unless otherwise noted all exhibits are from company records or reports.

than $50,000 specifying its expected payback period (from the date the project became operational to the repayment of the original investment) and projecting the anticipated return-on-funds employed (using average flows from the first 3, 5 and 10 years of the project's life). The policy ruled explicitly that any new venture's report must include deductions for anticipated incremental losses to *other* General Foods products occasioned by the new project. Top management generally required a *specified* projected 10 year average profit before taxes on invested funds, but it allowed the payback period to extend the full 10 years to cover losses accumulated during the market development period.

After reviewing the Product Group's profit projections and accompanying budget proposals, top management also bore the responsibility for weighing several factors: (1) duration of the period until break-even, (2) risks, (3) probable competition, (4) quality of forecasts, (5) period of greatest investment.

THE COFFEE MARKET

Coffee was, without question, the American national drink (see Exhibits 3 and 4). Coffee's position as the largest single beverage category was achieved by a broad demographic appeal and an ability to meet many needs and serve many functions. Thus coffee was seen by many consumers as being appropriate for most social occasions and at almost every time of day (see Exhibits 3 and 4).

A series of inquiries into the general motivational structure that indicated salient consumer needs and desires for the best cup of coffee were of considerable value in the development of freeze-dried coffee. Coffee was perceived as having a wide latitude of functions beyond satisfying thirst or providing warmth and comfort. The functions varied as to time of day, mood of the individual and particular needs at any given time. Some of these functions were: (1) a force to provide energy or stimulation, (2) a tension reliever with an implicit reward and consequently an aid to mental health, (3) a convenience food and a "snack," (4) an appetite-depressant, (5) a medication (with apparent emetic qualities) and (6) a "friend" in and of itself. Also coffee served as a visible symbol of adulthood.

Drinking coffee was universally associated with the sociability of a friendly gathering. Other perceptions of the coffee drinking situation were (1) an opportunity to relax, (2) a thought lubricator to help achieve concentrated thought, and (3) an excuse for sociability. The coffee break had an almost unique status as a reward for work well done, or as a legitimate escape from routinized drudgery.

Although consumers perceived coffee in a variety of ways, most agreed on what constituted the important attributes in a cup of coffee. These attributes, ranked according to the number of times they were mentioned, are shown below for two different ways of viewing the attributes:

	Attributes Desired in Everyday Cup of Coffee (Percent)	Attributes Needing Improvement for the Perfect Cup of Coffee (Percent)
Flavor/taste	62	37
Freshness	46	24
Good aroma	44	21
Gives you a lift	37	18
Relaxing	35	16
Strength without bitterness	30	22

Most consumers described their optimum cup of coffee as slightly s' rich yet smooth, with a minimum of calories.

Because coffee played so many roles so often, a major concern with regard to ground coffee was the bother of preparation—that is, the time consumed in preparation and the bother of cleaning the pot and disposing of the grounds. Also cited by consumers was their inability to achieve a consistently good cup of coffee, whether ground or soluble.

Size and Growth of Coffee Market

During the late fifties and early sixties, the combined instant and ground coffee market saw a period of consecutive increases well in excess of the 1.5 percent growth rate of the coffee drinking population (e.g., 14 years old and over). This growth can be traced to the introduction of a high quality soluble coffee in the early 1950's—Instant Maxwell House, and subsequently, to a general improvement in product quality for other soluble coffees, plus a limited amount of price elasticity.

Soluble coffees provided ease of preparation and made it convenient for people to serve coffee more frequently during the day. From 1950 to 1963, between meal coffee drinking doubled while meal-time coffee drinking showed small change (see Exhibit 5). Even though the between-meal convenience of soluble coffee came at some expense of flavor and aroma, its ease of preparation apparently weighed heavily enough to lead to its rapid adoption.

By 1962 instant coffee had added 0.67 cups per day to the average coffee intake while regular coffee had gained 0.14 cups per day (see Exhibits 5–7). Figures also show that the rapid growth of soluble consumption abetted the growth of the total industry until the soluble ratio[22] stood at 30.0 percent in 1964 (see Exhibit 8). This soluble ratio represented a slight decrease from the high of 31.6 percent in 1960.

Market Segmentation

Associated with the complexity of coffee buying and consumption were significant variations from the population norm in the behavior patterns of coffee drinking consumers. Maxwell House marketing executives divided the coffee market as follows:

By user type	Predominantly ground
	predominantly soluble
	dual users
By geographic area	East
	West
By size of urban area	Over 1,000,000 TV homes
	250,000 to 1,000,000 TV homes
	75,000 to 250,000 TV homes
	under 75,000 TV homes

The usefulness of this analysis came from the very different patterns of coffee drinking displayed in the East and West. Traditionally, Westerners drank more cups per day than Easterners. Consequently, since light coffee users had converted to instant coffee most readily, the Eastern soluble ratio (i.e., soluble/regular units purchased) greatly exceeded that in the West. The East, more populous by half, accounted for half again as many unit sales of soluble. Correspondingly, it contained more densely settled urban areas; cities with over 250,000 TV homes made up 75 percent of its population, while, in the more thinly settled West, they composed 64 percent of the populace. This was important for the introduction of new General Foods' products since

---

[22] The *soluble ratio* was the percent of total coffee volume (in units) accounted for by soluble coffee. This ratio is broken down by areas in Exhibit 16.

high-quality food innovations seemed to be adopted more readily in the larger urban areas. Exhibits 9 through 13 present the data which Maxwell House had collected to illuminate this market segmentation.

COMPETITIVE POSITION OF THE MAXWELL HOUSE DIVISION AND THE POSITIONING OF ITS BRANDS

In 1964, General Foods had a substantial share of the coffee market. Maxwell House Division marketed Sanka, Yuban and Maxwell Coffees nationally in both instant and regular form, consciously aiming each brand at a distinct consumer need to avoid "cannibalizing" sales to the extent possible.

Exhibits 14 through 16 indicate the strength of the Division's competitive position. Its soluble offerings commanded approximately 50 percent market share in both the East and the West and Instant Maxwell House sold more than three times as well as its nearest competitor. General Foods regular coffees enjoyed a 36 percent share of the Eastern market and a 13.5 percent share of the "low soluble" West, where they encountered strong competition from well-established regional brands.

Sanka was marketed to consumers who sought a coffee that could claim to let them sleep by virtue of its low caffeine content—a selling point that sharply distinguished Sanka from Yuban and Maxwell House. Since Sanka's share of the total coffee market was about 4 percent, and research indicated that about one coffee drinker in three was "concerned" about his caffein intake, there remained a considerable potential market for the Sanka brand. The major barrier to increased usage was the belief by most prospects that it was not real coffee and did not taste as good as "real" coffee. Thus Sanka tended to be used as a supplement to the usual coffee consumed, rather than as the primary coffee.

Yuban Coffee had been developed and introduced as a premium coffee differing from other brands in flavor and price. Ground Yuban had a flavor judged by consumers to be richer and more full-bodied than other ground coffees; Instant Yuban's flavor was judged to be "bitter/burnt" and more like that of ground coffee than competitive soluble brands. Ground Yuban sold at about a 10 percent premium at retail over most manufacturers' brands and Instant Yuban sold at about a 20 percent premium over most other soluble brands. Ground Yuban had been on the market for some years and in 1964 held 1.2 percent of the total coffee market, or about 1.8 percent of the ground coffee market. Instant Yuban had been introduced in 1959 in selected areas and expansion of its geographical coverage had been continuing since then. By 1964, Instant Yuban had achieved a 1.5 percent share of the total coffee market or 4.2 percent of the soluble coffee market.

In 1964, attempts were underway to reposition Yuban to replace its exotic and sophisticated, but apparently unsociable and strange, image with a warm and personable approach designed to establish it as a friendly coffee. The new plan aimed Yuban at the market segment that desired a coffee to please discriminating tastes and could (or would) afford to pay premium prices. Its product planners expected Yuban to attract older (30–50 years), better educated people in the higher income groups (upper 50 percent). Instant Yuban achieved its greatest franchise in the West and Northeast by claiming to be more ground-like than other instants (see Exhibit 16).

Regular Maxwell House, designed to appeal to the majority of ground coffee users, was sold at popular prices. A promotional goal was to achieve maximum loyalty through intensely competitive promotional programs, including strong consumer advertising. For this brand, the Division wished to develop a stronger franchise in the low soluble West where it faced stiff competition from regional brands like Hills and Folger's that had captured strong loyalty. It also sought a way to attract more young users (aged 18–25) to insure its long range market position.

Instant Maxwell House paralleled Regular Maxwell House by offering quality at a popular price and by claiming greater value than any other soluble coffee. As a foil to the potentially devastating effects of price dealing, Instant Maxwell House continually sought an improved blend which would increase consumer loyalty. The Division had also introduced a new 14-ounce jar in an effort to maintain consumer interest and to increase time between purchases so that the consumer might be less responsive to competitive promotion. To increase the number of Instant Maxwell House users in the West, the Division used heavy sampling and represented Instant Maxwell House as offering the "optimum coffee experience."

Price deals were used by Maxwell House management primarily as a defensive measure to prevent competitive retail prices from getting so far below Instant Maxwell House that previously loyal users would be lost. They were used less frequently to provide extra value inducements to encourage switching to Instant Maxwell House.

In general, soluble coffee marketers were putting more emphasis on promotions and less emphasis on media advertising (see Exhibit 17). The majority of the promotional dollars were going to off-label deals.[23] By 1964, sales on off-label promotions accounted for an estimated 50 percent of Folger's soluble sales, 80 percent of Nescafé's soluble sales and 30 percent of Maxwell House soluble sales.

DEVELOPMENT OF FREEZE-DRIED COFFEE

Through the middle and late 1950's, the Maxwell House Division had experimented with the use of a special freeze-drying process to produce a new type of soluble coffee. The Division's product planners began to focus increased attention on the still embryonic project in 1960, assigning it a top priority spot.

The freeze-drying process, the heart of the new development, closely resembled a technology long used by pharmaceutical firms. It produced a soluble coffee with a unique set of product characteristics. More concentrated than conventional instant coffee, crystalline in appearance, and soluble even in cold water, it offered flavor which rivalled that of regular ground coffee in consumer appeal.

The freeze-drying process began much like other techniques for manufacturing coffee: The manufacturer roasted and ground a carefully selected blend of green coffee beans. Then, as in the preparation of other soluble coffee, he brewed a strong coffee solution at a pressure and temperature somewhat higher than those found in normal home preparation. The next step differed radically from all other coffee-making techniques. At this point, the manufacturer flash-froze the solution. He subjected the resulting solid to a vacuum, and into this vacuum he suddenly introduced just enough local warmth to cause "sublimation" of the frozen solution's liquid content. "Sublimation," a kind of super-evaporation, resulted in a solid (ice) becoming a gas (water vapor) without passing through the liquid state. After this dehydration of the frozen coffee solution, the remaining sponge-like solids were ground up to ready them for packaging as soluble coffee.

This process departed entirely from the two more traditional techniques. The home-brewed method, used to prepare regular ground coffee, required only the first stages of the manufacturing process (blending, roasting and

---

[23]The term "off-label" referred to special tags or over-printing on labels, offering a special price reduction. In promotions of this type the manufacturers absorbed the drop in price and retailers received their regular dollar profit margin.

grinding) after which the user brewed the coffee himself in a percolator or dripolator at standard atmospheric pressure, with water heated to the boiling point (212°F). Consumers have long regarded coffee prepared in this manner as the standard for good taste and aroma.

The spray-dried method, formerly used to manufacture all instant coffees, required similar initial preparation. But the sealed brewing system worked at super-normal pressure and temperature to make the solution dense enough to afford a profitable yield. When this liquid was sprayed into a column of hot air in a drying tower, its coffee content fell to the bottom in a fine soluble powder ready for packaging. The spray-drying process reduced the coffee's flavor and aroma somewhat.

Freeze-dried coffee suffered from the first of these disadvantages less than did spray-dried, since its brewing did not require such intense heat. And there its flavor loss ended. The freeze-drying process saved the coffee from further flavor loss that occurred when spray-dried coffee entered the drying tower. Freeze-dried coffee, therefore, closely resembled ground coffee in flavor and aroma. The following chart summarizes these and other differences that resulted from the freeze-drying process:

	Spray-Dried Coffee	Freeze-Dried Coffee
Flavor	Less quality than regular, no astringency or "mouth feel"	Comparable to regular, some astringency, but less than regular
Aroma	Very little in cup aroma	Resembles regular in cup
Appearance	Powder	Irregular crystals
Solubility	Fair in cold water, foam in cup (due to air trapped in drying)	Good even in cold water little foam in cup
Concentration (weight per unit volume)	Index = 100	Index = 125
Cost per ounce	Index = 100	Index = 135

Freeze-dried coffee performed well when subject to blind cup taste tests. The following figures show disguised, but representative figures from two blind taste tests:[24]

Percent Preferring Maxim Versus . . .

Instant Maxwell House (Sample of 400 Soluble Users) (Percent)	Ground Maxwell House (Sample of 340 Ground Users) (Percent)
47	44

DEVELOPMENT OF A MARKETING STRATEGY

To make the planning task more manageable, the new products group assigned to freeze-dry coffee first identified the following basic operating assumptions:

1. That the finished product would possess the flavor of regular coffee and the convenience of instant,

2. That its advertising could make this claim credible,

---

[24] In both these tests about 14 percent of the sample expressed no preference.

3. That it would receive backing from advertising expenditures comparable to those invested in other new General Foods products and that these would insure its domination of coffee advertising media,

4. That the product would succeed in maintaining the margin set for it.

These assumptions were necessary to provide a starting point for the setting of goals, to put some constraints on the development of feasible price, advertising, promotion and position alternatives, and to guide the consumer research program.

Secondly, Mr. Carter arranged a series of meetings with senior division and corporate executives to review these operating assumptions and to clarify what was expected of the new product. For the most part these performance expectations were based on requirements for a recognizable success. But success in this context was not merely achieving designated financial goals for the product itself; it also required that the new product should not prosper at the expense of other company brands.

The operating assumptions and the following performance expectations guided the thinking of the new product group during most of 1963. However, as the time came to solidify the marketing plan, some of these guides looked to be in conflict with others, or obsolete in terms of new evidence collected during 1963. Any changes made would have to be justified since the modified form would serve as the operating goal and performance criteria for the new product. Mr. Carter also suspected that it would be quite hard to have the expectations scaled down if subsequent research, planning and market experience showed them to be unreasonable.

Performance Expectations

The following are the expectations that guided the initial planning of the freeze-dry coffee strategy:

A. The franchise would be built outside that currently held by other Division products.

B. The gross margin would be at least equal to that on comparable products and better than that on cannibalized business. This was necessary to help pay for the enormous investment in new plant and equipment.

C. The product should endeavor to increase the soluble ratio, particularly in the West.

D. The benefits of the freeze-dried process would be exploited before competition broadly marketed a comparable product.

Underlying these explicit expectations was a basic requirement that the new coffee achieve a going year franchise (expressed in terms of share of the soluble coffee market plus people converted from ground to freeze-dried) that would generate enough volume to meet corporate return on funds employed criteria for new products—and still support a campaign that would dominate coffee advertising media.

The product manager's estimate of the going year franchise, and ultimately its acceptance as a reasonable performance objective, required some very difficult judgments with respect to:

1. The probable rate at which regular and instant users would convert to the new product. A major question concerned the degree to which the "soluble stigma" would make ground users more difficult to convert.

2. The variation in the franchise by market size. The range of the variation would depend somewhat on the extent to which the product was

perceived as a premium coffee. Experience with premium priced coffees such as Yuban showed that the larger urban markets would be more receptive to such an innovation. The question was: how much more receptive? The answer to this question would also weigh heavily in deciding media allocations by market size and type.

3. The effect of the various performance expectations, which are discussed in more detail below:

Build a Franchise Outside That Currently Held by Other Division Products. Because the Division already commanded about half of the instant coffee market in both East and West, a sizeable share of the Eastern business would inevitably come from *other* Maxwell House Brands. Nevertheless, the greatest profits obviously lay in attracting those who had not previously used a General Foods coffee, since this new franchise would directly expand the company's volume and market share. Conversion of customers from other brands was, therefore, of primary importance.

In projecting profit figures for various marketing plans, Mr. Carter needed a device to predict the comparative likelihood of gains in company franchise as opposed to mere cannibalization. The simplest model considered was one which assumed that the new coffee's usage would come from all other brands in exact proportion to their previously existing market share (in units). Thus if Brand X currently held a 12 percent share of the Eastern soluble market, the new coffee would gain 12 percent of its Eastern soluble target from this brand. Other more complex "cannibalization" models were also considered. Their usefulness was limited because of the lack of evidence that they were any improvement over the simple model.

Maintain a Gross Margin Higher Than That on Cannibalized Business. The logic of the simple model determined that if Instant Maxwell House commanded 38 percent of the Eastern soluble market, the new product would steal 38 percent of its Eastern soluble target from Instant Maxwell House. So, in order to insure the Division an incremental profit to help pay for the tremendous investment required to produce freeze-dried coffee, Mr. Carter suggested establishing a requirement that the gross margin on the new coffee must exceed that on Instant Maxwell House ($2.50 per unit) which in turn already exceeded that on Regular Maxwell House ($2.00 per unit). The higher margin on IMH over RMH reflected the greater cost for plant and equipment required to produce this form of coffee and the need to develop a reasonable return on this investment. This meant that, within reasonable limits which did not distort the scale of production on the Division's other offering, incremental profits would result even from stealing Maxwell House customers.

Increase the Soluble Ratio, Particularly in the West. The conversion of regular coffee buyers to use of the new soluble coffee was a more profitable prospect than the conversion of instant users for two reasons:

1. The Division commanded a lower market share among regular users, particularly in the West, so that conversion of regular users produced cannibalization with fewer drawbacks than did the conversion of instant users (see Exhibit 14).

2. Even where the Division's new product cannibalized its own brands, the margin on instant coffee ($2.50 per unit) exceeded that on regular ($2.00 per unit), making conversion of the latter the more profitable prospect (by $0.50 per unit).

Exploit the Freeze-drying Process before the Competition Broadly Markets a Comparable Product. Since the Division had spent years developing its new coffee product at a time when the question of its eventual practicability remained uncertain, it had necessarily borne the expense of such exploratory research which competitors would not need to repeat. Naturally, the Division wished to reap the rewards of its advantage by establishing a strongly loyal franchise before competitors could enter the market.

Mr. Carter estimated that it would take at least two years for any company to develop an offering of comparable quality and make it operational. Following that, it would be at least another year before the competitor had acquired enough production capacity to be able to go national. He reported that while anyone could produce limited quantities of freeze-dried coffee in the laboratory, transferring the technique to a mass production scale posed difficult problems that required at least two years to solve. He added that, even then, only a major coffee producer could handle such an operation.

Nevertheless, the manufacturing process, having served pharmaceutical firms for years, remained unpatentable. The situation, therefore, presented the danger that, after cannibalizing some of the Division's share, the new brand might then lose share to some especially successful and aggressive freeze-dried competitor with the net result that the Maxwell House Division's total share could actually decline.

Rumors in the trade indicated that one major international competitor (Nestlé) and a very few small, North American firms were experimenting with—and were about ready to test, on a limited scale—freeze-dried, concentrated coffees. The quantity and quality of these possible competitive coffees were unknown. Of the firms in question it seemed highly probable that only the Nestlé company had the technical skill and financial resources necessary to market successfully a freeze-dried concentrated coffee. An interesting aspect of the rumors was the purported Nestlé strategy—to direct its freeze-dried coffee entirely against the soluble market. It would then cannibalize from Nescafé as well as attempt to take a share from all other solubles.

On a national level, the competitive position of General Foods' innovation depended on the company's ability to achieve enough capacity to serve a national market. Mr. Carter estimated that new plants could achieve additional volume at the rate of 2 million annual units per $10 million investment at an operating cost of $5.72 per 48-ounce unit[25] (this cost does not include depreciation). Each plant would take at least a year to build, plus several months to reach capacity volume. While the minimum plant size was two million units, plants could be built to any capacity up to a maximum of four million units. The operating cost per unit was expected to be the same regardless of the capacity.

ACHIEVING THE GOALS

Mr. Carter recognized that the stringent performance expectations could only be met if the Division's marketing efforts found an effective set of appeals to give Maxim a favorable market "position." This meant that he had to decide first what image to seek for the new product, then he had to select a name, a label, a package, and other product features that would successfully conjure up this image in the public eye, and finally he had to decide how to allocate advertising and promotional funds for efficient attainment of these positioning goals.

Positioning

The initial expectations of the new product suggested that it meet the following positioning requirements:

---

[25] A unit is a fractional composite made up of:

6	—	four-ounce jars
4.8	—	two-ounce jars
1.8	—	eight-ounce jars

which equals 48 ounces of Maxim. This is the basic unit of analysis.

1. That it be assigned to a unique position, clearly different from the positions of the Division's existing brands, so as to minimize cannibalization.

2. That it be differentiated from both other types of coffee so as to establish it as a new *form* of coffee; a third type which offers ground users their customary flavor with new convenience and which allows instant users to retain ease of preparation while improving the taste of their brew.

3. That it be an extension to the Maxwell House line rather than a completely new brand name.

Mr. Carter recognized, however, that the threefold objectives of assigning the coffee a unique position, differentiating it from all others, and registering its association with Maxwell House, while difficult enough to achieve in themselves, complicated the situation still further by conflicting with each other at several points. For example, the more the package emphasized the connection between the new coffee and Maxwell House (a fulfillment of the third goal), the more it encouraged the probability of substitution between the two (a violation of the first). And so, Mr. Carter had to handle several dilemmas to achieve the best possible balance among these three goals.

Name

To balance these positioning requirements Mr. Carter sought a name which would provide an optimum association with Maxwell House without producing so close an identity that substitution would occur to an undesirable degree. Before making his recommendation, he considered two concepts:[26]

1. Using the Maxwell House name directly with some modifier attached,

2. Using a separate brand name that implied its parentage with only minor emphasis.

For the second concept he considered several alternatives, finally narrowing the choice to three—Prima, Nova, and Maxim. A study, asking 463 women respondents to report their association with these names and rate them on various scales, produced the results given in Exhibit 19.

Alternatives based on the first concept included Maxwell House Coffee Concentrate, Maxwell House Concentrated Soluble Coffee, and Maxwell House Concentrated Instant Coffee. Of these, Mr. Carter preferred the first or second for their distinctiveness since research had shown them to be relatively unfamiliar to the consumer (see Exhibit 20). Mr. Carter rejected the first concept altogether because he felt that use of the Maxwell House name under these circumstances would merely attract current Division patrons rather than new users. He disliked the second concept because of consumer unfamiliarity with the term soluble. Moreover, reassuring evidence came from a study which indicated that a separate brand name could generate almost as much consumer interest as the familiar "Maxwell House." Subjects who were offered a choice between three gifts—(1) Instant Maxwell House, (2) Regular Maxwell House, or (3) one of four competing alternative names—chose Maxim or Prima over 50% of the time, an acceptable frequency in Mr. Carter's judgment (see Exhibit 20).

Mr. Carter tentatively chose "Maxim" because of its easy association with coffee (22%) and favorable connotations,[27] pointing out that "Maxim": (1)

---

[26] These two basic concepts were subject to some further modifications according to the kind of descriptive designation associated with the chosen brand name (see Exhibits 18–21).

[27] See Exhibit 19.

Implies concentration and strength (index = 132), (2) connotates quality and superiority (37% and index = 135), (3) relates to Maxwell House (33%), and (4) is short, memorable and euphonious. However, not everyone was equally convinced that Maxim was the best choice, particularly because of the association with Maxwell House.

Jar Size and Design

Mr. Carter recommended packing Maxim in 2-ounce, 4-ounce and 8-ounce sizes. He expected the 2-ounce size to encourage purchase on a trial basis, to expand Maxim's shelf facings, and to return a higher margin than other sizes. He selected the 4-ounce size to enable Maxim to offer the consumer a middle-sized jar with price and cup yield comparable to a pound of ground coffee (about 50 cups at under a dollar). He counted on the 8-ounce size to offer convenience and economy to heavy users and to attain a price comparable to other brands' large sizes.

As a further aid in distinguishing Maxim from all other brands, the packaging department designed a jar that differed markedly from everything else on the market. Oval instead of round, it faced the buyer with a shouldered, rectangular shape, topped by a special lug-screw cap with separate label panels instead of the customary wrap-around labeling Tests showed that this shape was superior to either a square or a round alternative in generating product interest (see Exhibit 22).

Copy Strategy

Mr. Carter proposed a copy strategy which grew out of his conviction that Maxim did indeed present an inherently superior product, combining the best features of traditional regular and instant coffees and eliminating many of the defects of both. He and his subordinates believed that Maxim's advertising must be directed to (1) convince ground users that they could continue to enjoy fine coffee flavor with new convenience, and (2) to persuade instant users that they could now make a soluble brew that tasted like regular ground coffee.

To assign Maxim a position as a new type of coffee with the taste of regular and the convenience of instant, he planned to present the new entry as *being* real percolated coffee, the result of a scientific breakthrough which enabled freeze-dried coffee literally to *become* fresh perked coffee in the buyer's cup.

To overcome the slightly incredible aura of this claim, the copy strategy called for several reinforcing features. It counted on the freeze-dried process story as its "reason-why." Tangibly, the coffee's granular form would help establish it as a new type of coffee; and hopefully, the newness suggested by this crystalline shape would help reduce the "soluble stigma" that might otherwise contradict the claim to superior flavor. At the same time, the messages would offer the buyer reassurance through emphasis on the coffee's high quality and by alluding to its connection with Maxwell House—an association which would strengthen the suggestion of quality and lend an atmosphere of authority. Finally, the copy strategy proposed to reinforce Maxim's singular position by pointing to its concentration, i.e., the greater weight per unit volume. The buyer needed to use less, a characteristic which should connote both quality and economy (moreover, the consumer must recognize this fact when preparing his cupful to avoid excessively strong taste).

Assuming this was the best copy strategy to follow Mr. Carter then faced the problem of selecting the best means of translating it into complete advertisements. Two executions of the copy strategy submitted by the advertising agency for consideration by Mr. Carter are shown in Attachment 1 along with associated testing.

Advertising Budget

Mr. Carter felt that the adoption of the operating assumption that Maxim should dominate coffee advertising logically implied the following media objectives:

1. *To direct weight against all coffee users 18 and over, especially house-wives in households with incomes above $3,500.*

Experience with other products had suggested that those with incomes below $3,500 would hesitate to accept a premium-priced, high quality food product like Maxim. In a test conducted to determine the chief source of coffee buying decisions, the housewife proved to have made the choice entirely on her own in at least 65 percent of the instant-using homes and in at least 61 percent of the ground-using homes (see Exhibit 23).

2. *To provide weight sufficient to stimulate maximum trial and repeat usage.*

3. *To achieve media dominance within the soluble coffee category.*

In this respect, the plan "aimed to insure the consumer's attention and aware-ness of Maxim's introduction by saturating coffee-promoting media in each area in an effort to make Maxim the most salient new food product in the public consciousness."

New product advertising was typically divided into three periods—a two-week *stocking* period (to stimulate consumer—and trade—interest so as to insure adequate distribution), a 26-week *introductory* period (to create awareness, encourage trial, and provide reinforcement to secure repurchase), a 20-week *sustaining* period to retain initial triers and extend brand awareness over introductory goals).

The final advertising budget, for the first year, had to be built from these general considerations in a step-by-step process:

1. Since it was assumed that no product trial would come without con-sumer awareness of the new brand, an awareness objective had to be set for each advertising period. Experience with other comparable new products showed that an overall awareness of at least 60 percent had to be achieved, by the end of the introductory period, if the product was to be successful.

2. The awareness goals needed to be scaled by market size and by shares expected in those areas. Since bigger shares were expected to come from larger urban markets, the awareness objectives should be corre-spondingly higher. A reasonable range of awareness objectives is shown below.[28]

---

[28] Reasonable share and awareness objectives during introductory period:

Market Size (TV Homes)	Estimated Maximum and Minimum Feasible Awareness (Percent of TV Homes)
Over 1,000,000	65—75%
250,000 to 1,000,000	60—70
75,000 to 250,000	50—60
0—75,000	40—60

3. A critical step would be the conversion of awareness goals into estimates of reach and frequency (that is, the cumulative audience, and the number of repeated messages being delivered to the cumulative audience). Sufficient impact during the introductory period could probably be generated in the largest markets with a reach of 80–90 percent and a frequency of once per week. During the sustaining period the frequency usually was cut by half or more. Also a budget at this sustaining level could probably suffice for the second year. Some adjustments might have to be made during the campaign to combat competitive advertising efforts. Usually this meant out-spending the competition by shifting funds into the period of heaviest competitive advertising.

4. There was little question that spot television would be the basic medium to be used. It was already the common media practice in the coffee industry; absorbing an estimated 59 percent of the industry's 1963 budget. Another 20 percent of the industry budget went to network television expenditures.

5. A final problem, resulting from the desire to increase the soluble ratio, was the relative allotment to the high and low soluble areas. The expenditure of the same number of dollars per capita in both areas would certainly result in regional disproportions in terms of dollars per units sold. The question was how far out of line was the extra expenditure per unit sold in the low soluble area?

Adherence to the initial assumptions of awareness, reach, frequency and media for the purpose of an "order of magnitude" estimate of the advertising investment produced an expenditure range of $9,500,000 to $12,500,000 in the first year and $6,000,000 to $7,000,000 in the second year. This clearly ensured media dominance (see Exhibit 24) but did not answer questions of adequacy or inadequacy.

Promotions

As a general policy for Maxim, Mr. Carter urged the principle that wherever possible the brand should direct promotion at the consumer rather than the dealer. He believed that the industry had subscribed to too many trade incentives, many of which proved ineffective, and preferred promotional offers such as free containers, free jars for two innerseals, free enclosed premiums, and so on—offers which exerted "pull-through" by establishing direct contact with the consumer. This, of course, ruled out off-label dealing, which often lost its impact before reaching the consumer. However, some sort of introductory trade allowance and display offer would be necessary in order to ensure rapid distribution. Based on past experience, a trade promotion budget of at least $3,500,000 would be needed to ensure 80 to 85 percent distribution by the end of the 26 week introductory period.

A great deal of emphasis was placed on a promotional plan that would secure broad product trial. There was a strong belief that a buyer's experience with Maxim would result in a high level of satisfaction and that this was the best way to overcome inhibitions resulting from Maxim's premium price, or the "soluble stigma."

To obtain cost estimates Mr. Carter asked several large promotion houses to quote on the following promotional alternatives:

1. Two-ounce samples with 25 cent repurchase coupon delivered door-to-door

2. Mailed coupons redeemable for free jar

3. Mailed packets of six individually measured servings with a 25 cent repurchase coupon.

The restriction placed on the quotes was that only urban homes with incomes over $3,500[29] be considered, in accord with the basic media objectives. One quotation, based on sending just a coupon to the smaller urban areas (which had an eligible population of 9,000,000 households), is shown in Exhibit 25. This left Mr. Carter with the problem of deciding what combination of samples, coupons and populations should be adopted. For example, if a coupon (redeemable for a free jar) were sent to all 34,000,000 households the cost would be $12,400,000, but a 2-ounce jar and 25 cent coupon would cost $16,050,000 if sent to all households. Other combinations of samples and coupons were also possible.

Pricing

Pricing presented particularly sticky problems. In the first place, Mr. Carter could not hope to set a definite or permanent price for Maxim before actually entering the market, simply because the price of coffee imports had long showed a confirmed tendency to fluctuate violently—by as much as 10 to 20 percent a year—and retail prices for the entire coffee market reflected these fluctuations. Consequently, Mr. Carter tended to view the Maxim pricing decision in terms of (a) Maxim's premium over Instant Maxwell House and other Division brands and (b) the margin generated after accounting for the retailer's mark-up

Several other difficulties already mentioned above made the decision for pricing Maxim particularly tough. First, freeze-dried coffee cost about 35 percent more to make than the equivalent weight of spray-dried. Secondly, pricing had to reflect a result of business it took away from the Division's other brands. Thirdly, Maxim's concentrated form made the per cup premium apply to a smaller total volume per ounce. This meant that a smaller jar could be used for 2-ounce, 4-ounce and 8-ounce sizes, a confusion which might affect the consumer's perception—either favorably or unfavorably.

Indeed, Mr. Carter faced what he felt to be a sharply-pronged dilemma, for he realized that with the coffee market's high price elasticity Maxim might not realize its market share goals (especially for ground user conversion) if it were priced at a differential high enough to bring an incremental profit on cannibalized business.

To aid in clarifying the position, several alternative price structures were drawn up—each with a different margin and a different premium relationship to Instant Maxwell House and other Division brands. Discussion was not limited to the price structure shown in Exhibits 26 and 27; nor was everyone willing to consider these two prices to be the extremes that were possible. Those who were more concerned with the market's price elasticity generally favored the price structure shown in Exhibit 26. This structure would establish a premium relationship to Instant Maxwell House of 12.2 percent/28.8 percent/43.0 percent for the 2-, 4-, and 8-ounce sizes respectively, and would yield a higher margin to reflect high investment in plant and equipment. The per cup cost to the consumer would be close to that of Regular Maxwell House.[30]

A second alternative with a great deal of support was based on the feeling that a higher premium such as 16.3 percent/40 percent/51.9 percent (see

---

[29]This was a total of 34 million homes, of which 25 million were in major urban areas. This excluded 23 million homes that were either in rural areas or had incomes less than $3,500.

[30] Per cup costs were computed on the assumption that both spray-dried and freeze-dried coffee would yield the same number of cups per ounce. However, since Maxim was more concentrated the volume per cup would be smaller.

Exhibit 27) would not injure consumer acceptance of Maxim. This prediction came from the view that Maxim, as an inherently superior product, might show less price sensitivity than other coffees. On the other hand, the Yuban experience showed that it was harder to gain trade support for premium priced coffees. This was in spite of the fact that retailers would require a margin of 13 percent of the retail price, regardless of the price level chosen.

A further alternative, with some potential legal drawbacks, was to price Maxim lower in the West. The desired result was to lure a larger number of ground users, since the Division had less to fear from cannibalization.

Choice of Alternatives

The final decision on the price level was bound up with the concurrent decisions on positioning, advertising and promotion. The approach used to consider the logical combinations of these elements was to create a "pro forma" share, budget and profit projection for each combination.

However, before these projections could be made, a number of problem areas had to be resolved:

1. The gross margin and cost projections could be tentatively established from the requirement that Maxim demand a margin greater than that of other Maxwell House coffees.

2. A more difficult problem concerned the state of the market to be expected in the three years following the introduction. Three years was a typical planning horizon for the financial evaluation of a new food product. But even this period was long when it came to estimating future sales trends and competitive responses.

3. A broader policy question concerned the effect of the reduced sales volume of other Division brands (because of Maxim cannibalization) on the advertising and promotion budgets of these brands. If these budgets were fixed at 1963 levels the rest of the Division would lose its entire margin on each unit cannibalized. This loss would have to be charged to Maxim profits. On the other hand, if these advertising and promotion budgets were reduced in proportion to the decrease in sales, the incremental loss to the rest of the Division would be limited to the customary net profit per unit.

ATTACHMENT 1
ALTERNATIVE EXECUTIONS OF THE COPY STRATEGY

Ogilvy, Benson & Mather prepared two television commercials embodying the general copy points outlined above, each with a somewhat different emphasis. The "Freeze-dried Announcement" stressed the effectiveness of the innovative manufacturing discovery; the "Perfect Percolator Cup" concentrated on the claim that Maxim tastes even better than ground coffee because it has no bitter aftertaste. The agency tested each ad with forced in-home trials. O. B. & M. also submitted two newspaper advertisements (one of which included a 10 cent coupon) stressing the theme that freeze-drying produces a crystalline coffee with the power to turn every cup into a percolator. The agency further suggested outdoor and transit displays proclaiming first "Maxim Is Coming" and then "Maxim Is Here."

Freeze-dried Announcement

ANNOUNCER: You are looking at an entirely new form of coffee. You are looking at freeze-dried coffee. Tiny, concentrated crystals that have the power to turn every cup in your house into a percolator! This is Maxim, the entirely new form of coffee from Maxwell House. After years of research, it was discovered that freshly brewed coffee could be frozen. The ice could be drawn off in a vacuum, and you would have freeze-dried coffee, concentrated crystals of real percolated coffee. That's Maxim. Rich, full bodied, exactly like the finest coffee you ever brewed. Let Maxim turn every cup in your house into a percolator! Get Maxim, the entirely new form of coffee from Maxwell House.

(Accompanied by appropriate *sound effects*: crystals dropping into cup, water pouring, coffee perking, vacuum being applied, more water pouring and perking; and by appropriate *visual effects*: close-up of crystals on spoon, cup changing into percolator, close-up of jar, perked coffee being frozen and vacuumized, man savoring taste, close-up of label.)

Perfect Percolator Coffee

PRETTY YOUNG HOUSEWIFE: I make better coffee than you do. That's right. I make better coffee than you do. Without a coffee pot. Without a powdery instant coffee. (Slams cupboard door.) But *with* an entirely new kind of coffee! It's Maxim. (Close-up of jar.) And it's fantastic! Maxim turns every cup in your house into a percolator. (Cups turning into percolators.) Yes, Maxim makes better coffee right in the cup than you can brew in a coffee pot. Perfect percolator coffee with none of that harsh, bitter taste you sometimes get with ground.

ANNOUNCER: Maxim's secret? A totally new process from Maxwell House turns real percolated coffee into crystals. Tiny concentrated crystals with the power to turn every cup in your house into a percolator. (Repeat visual sequence of cups turning into percolators.)

PRETTY YOUNG HOUSEWIFE: That's why I make better coffee than you do. Unless you've discovered Maxim too.

ANNOUNCER: Maxim, the entirely new form of coffee from Maxwell House.

Test of "Freeze-dried Announcement" vs. "Perfect Percolator Cup"

	Freeze-dried Announcement		Perfect Percolator Cup	
	Immediate (Percent)	24-Hour (Percent)	Immediate (Percent)	24-Hour (Percent)
Recall:				
It's Frozen	63	72	—	—
It's Dehydrated, Dried	36	42	—	—
It's Perked, Brewed	26	22	4	4
It's Crystallized	18	14	40	40
8 Pots in One Jar	36	15	—	—
It's Concentrated	15	10	10	10
Tastes Like Real Perked	20	14	16	14
Can Make Better Coffee Than You	—	—	20	12
Turns Every Cup Into a Percolator	16	7	24	18
An Instant Coffee	18	8	24	26
Connotation:				
Maxim Different	84%		74%	
Reference to Process	46%		23	
Reference to Flavor	20		41	
Reference to New, Different	35		19	
About the Same	14		22	

EXHIBIT 1

General Foods Financial Statistics, Fiscal Years*
(all dollar amounts in millions, except assets per employee and figures on a share basis)

	1964 (Est.)	1963	1962	1961	1960	1959	1958
INCOME							
Sales to customers (net)	$1,338	$1,216	$1,189	$1,160	$1,087	$1,053	$1,009
Cost of sales	838	774	769	764	725	734	724
Marketing, administrative and general expenses	322	274	267	261	236	205	181
Earnings before income taxes	179	170	156	138	130	115	105
Taxes on income	95	91	84	71	69	61	57
Net earnings	84	79	72	67	61	54	48
Net earnings per common share	3.33	3.14	2.90	2.69	2.48	2.21	1.99
Dividends on common shares	50	45	40	35	32	28	24
Dividends per common share	2.00	1.80	1.60	1.40	1.30	1.15	1.00
Earnings retained in business each year	34	34	32	32	29	26	24
ASSETS, LIABILITIES, AND STOCKHOLDERS' EQUITY							
Current assets	$ 436	$ 411	$ 387	$ 360	$ 357	$ 329	$ 313
Current liabilities	202	162	142	123	126	107	107
Working capital	234	249	245	237	230	222	206
Land, buildings, equipment, gross	436	375	328	289	247	221	203
Land, buildings, equipment, net	264	223	193	173	148	132	125
Long-term debt	23	34	35	37	40	44	49
Stockholders' equity	490	454	419	384	347	315	287
Book value per common share	19.53	18.17	16.80	15.46	14.07	12.87	11.78
OPERATING STATISTICS							
Inventories	$ 256	$ 205	$ 183	$ 189	$ 157	$ 149	$ 169
Capital additions	70	57	42	40	35	24	28
Depreciation	26	24	21	18	15	14	11
Wages, salaries, and benefits	195	180	171	162	147	138	128
Number of employees (in thousands)	30	28	28	25	22	22	21
Assets per employee (in thousands)	24	23	22	22	23	22	21

*Fiscal 1964 ended April 2, 1964. Other fiscal years ended March 31.

EXHIBIT 2

Organizational Chart for Maxwell House Division

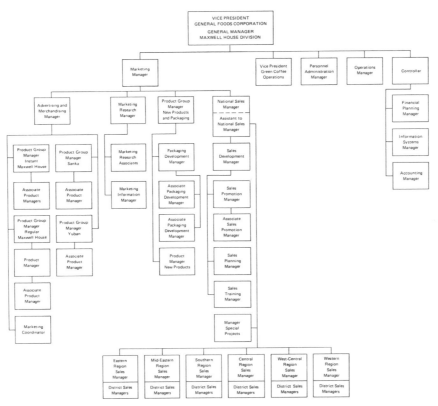

EXHIBIT 3

Consumption of Coffee and Other Beverages
(percentage of persons 10 years of age and over)

	1950	1962	1963
Coffee	74.7	74.7	73.2
Milk and milk drinks	51.0	52.6	52.3
Fruit and vegetable juices	32.8	41.4	38.3
Soft drinks	29.1	32.6	34.0
Tea	24.0	24.7	24.7
Cocoa, hot chocolate	5.4	4.5	4.0

EXHIBIT 4

Coffee's Share of Beverage Market
(Index 1961 = 100)

	Consumer $ Bases	Liquid Consumption Basis
1961	100	100
1962	95	98
1963	90	97

SOURCE: Maxwell House Market Research Department.

EXHIBIT 5

Trends in Coffee Drinking
(cups per person per day)

	Fiscal Year						
	1950	1953	1960	1961	1962	1963	1964 (Est.)
Regular:							
At home	N.A.	N.A.	1.78	1.90	1.95	1.93	1.86
At eating places	N.A.	N.A.	0.25	0.26	0.28	0.22	0.24
At work	N.A.	N.A.	0.18	0.17	0.22	0.21	0.19
Total Regular		2.31	2.21	2.33	2.45	2.36	2.29
Instant:							
At home	N.A.	N.A.	0.52	0.59	0.62	0.60	0.56
At eating places	N.A.	N.A.	0.00	0.01	0.01	0.00	0.00
At work	N.A.	N.A.	0.04	0.04	0.04	0.05	0.05
Total Instant		0.56	0.56	0.64	0.67	0.65	0.61
Breakfast	1.03	N.A.	1.11	1.18	1.17	1.18	1.14
Other meals	0.91	N.A.	0.89	0.92	0.98	0.90	0.85
Between meals	0.44	N.A.	0.77	0.87	0.97	0.93	0.91
Total for day	2.38	2.57	2.77	2.97	3.12	3.01	2.90

EXHIBIT 6

Coffee Drinking by Age Groups
(cups per person per day; percentage of age group drinking coffee)

| | 1950 | | 1962 | | 1963 | | 1964 (Est.) | | % Change 1950—64 | |
	Cups	Percent	Cups	Percent	Cups	Percent	Cups	Percent	Cups	Percent
10–14	0.21	(16.0)	0.18	(13.4)	0.18	(13.1)	0.18	(12.2)	–14.3	– 3.8
15–19	1.13	(53.8)	1.09	(40.2)	0.89	(37.1)	0.71	(31.7)	–37.2	–22.1
20–24	2.34	(75.2)	2.99	(76.6)	2.70	(69.1)	2.30	(68.4)	– 1.7	– 6.8
25–29	2.78	(83.3)	3.88	(85.2)	3.76	(81.4)	3.64	(84.3)	+30.9	+ 1.0
30–39	3.02	(87.4)	4.50	(88.8)	4.38	(89.7)	4.14	(85.8)	+37.1	– 1.6
40–49	2.98	(88.0)	4.44	(91.4)	4.27	(90.7)	4.33	(89.6)	+45.3	+ 1.6
50–59	2.85	(91.2)	3.83	(92.9)	3.75	(89.3)	3.68	(88.2)	+29.1	– 3.0
60–69	*2.22	(86.0)	3.01	(89.8)	3.17	(89.8)	3.06	(90.6)	—	—
70 and over			2.39	(85.8)	2.40	(86.8)	2.47	(88.7)	—	—

*Figures include all persons 60 years of age and older.

SOURCE: Pan-American Coffee Bureau, based on a national probability sample survey of 6,000 civilians over 10 years of age, taken at midwinter.

EXHIBIT 7

U.S. Per Capita Coffee Consumption, 1946–1964
(pounds per capita)

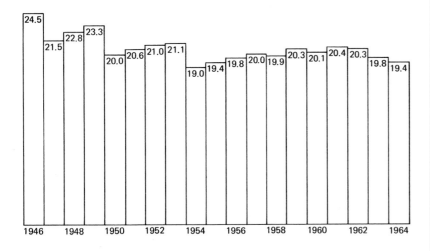

EXHIBIT 8

Coffee Consumption Trends, Fiscal 1955–1964

Fiscal Years	Total Coffee (000,000 lbs.)	Equivalent Units (000,000)	Soluble Ratio	Growth of Soluble Sales vs. Year Ago (Percent)	High Sol. East (000,000) Reg. Units	Sol. Units	Low Sol. West (000,000) Reg. Units	Sol. Units
1964 (est.)	2,102	174.5	30.0	– 2.1	63.0	38.2	59.1	14.2
1963	2,171	170.9	31.3	0.2	59.9	38.8	57.5	14.7
1962	2,163	168.8	31.6	5.6	58.4	38.9	57.0	14.5
1961	2,080	163.2	30.9	7.4	57.7	36.6	55.0	13.9
1960	1,984	155.9	30.1	5.3	55.4	33.6	53.5	13.4
1959	1,955	154.1	29.0	9.3	55.7	32.0	53.7	12.7
1958	1,863	147 5	27.7	19.4	54.3	29.3	52.3	11.6
1957	1,738	138.6	24.7	20.8	54.1	25.4	50.2	8.9
1956	1,654	131.5	21.6	21.5	54.8	21.2	48.3	7.2
1955	1,500	120.4	19.4	—	52.0	17.4	45.1	5.9

EXHIBIT 9

Coffee Drinking by Region
(cups per person per day)

	1950	1962	1963	(Est.) 1964	Percentage Change 1950–64
East	2.27	2.91	2.76	2.54	+11.9
Midwest	2.72	3.34	3.30	3.20	+17.6
South	1.91	2.78	2.54	2.61	+36.6
West	2.79	3.52	3.56	3.38	+21.1
U.S.A.	2.38	3.12	3.01	2.90	+21.8

SOURCE: Pan-American Coffee Bureau Annual Study.

EXHIBIT 10

Sales and Soluble Ratio by Area—Fiscal 1964 (Est.)

	East	West	Total U.S.
Population over 14 (000,000)	81.0	33.0	134.0
Total coffee market *(000,000 units)	101.2	73.3	174.5
Soluble ratio (Soluble/Total units)	42.9	22.9	30.0

*(Unit = 48-ounce soluble or 12-pounds ground)

EXHIBIT 11

Geographical Distribution of Coffee User Types

Type of Coffee	Total U.S. (Percent)	North-east (Percent)	South (Percent)	Mid-west (Percent)	West Central (Percent)	Pacific (Percent)
Ground only users	37	24	40	34	49	51
Users of both	48	57	35	52	42	32
Instant only users	15	19	25	14	9	7

EXHIBIT 12

Composition of the Coffee Market by User Type

	Percentage of Families (Percent)	Percentage of Coffee Volume (Percent)	Percentage of Regular Coffee Volume (Percent)	Percentage Of Instant Coffee Volume (Percent)
Exclusively Regular	48	54	76	2
Predominantly Regular (60–89 percent)	14	15	17	12
Instant and Regular (40–59 percent)	5	5	4	8
Predominantly Instant (60–89 percent)	10	8	3	20
Exclusively Instant	23	18	—	58

SOURCE: Maxwell House Market Research Department

EXHIBIT 13

Population by Size of Urban Area
(in 000s)

Number of TV Homes	East	West
Over 1 million	42,896	20,454
250,000—1,000,000	41,348	27,071
75,000—250,000	22,520	18,116
0—75,000	5,481	8,483
Total	112,245	74,124

EXHIBIT 14

Competitive Position—Fiscal 1964 (Est.)

	Percentage		
	East	West	Total U.S.
Division Share:			
Regular	36.0	13.5	24.9
Instant	50.7	47.1	50.3
Volume	76	24	100
Gross Profit	77	23	100
Advertising and Promotion	62	38	100
Merchandising Profit	84	16	100

EXHIBIT 15

Competitive Position—Fiscal 1964 (Est.)
(brand share)

Soluble Market	Percent	Ground Market	Percent
Instant Maxwell House	36.8	Regular Maxwell House	21.4
Nescafe	12.2	Folger's	15.1
Sanka	9.3	Hills	9.7
Chase and Sanborn	6.6	Chase and Sanborn	6.5
Folger's	5.9		
Yuban	4.2		

EXHIBIT 16

Soluble Ratio and Market Share by Region

	East	Mid-East	South	Central	West Central	West
Fiscal 1963						
Maxwell House:						
Instant	39.2	40.2	43.1	37.4	39.4	28.1
Regular	32.1	35.9	32.7	16.1	7.6	8.9
Yuban:						
Instant	7.6	3.3	2.6	2.4	0.8	7.9
Regular	2.2	1.2	0.8	0.5	0.1	4.8
Soluble Ratio	39.3	40.2	38.4	27.8	18.9	20.4
Fiscal 964 (Est.)						
Maxwell House:						
Instant	37.9	38.4	41.1	36.9	36.4	24.4
Regular	33.1	36.9	31.4	16.1	8.8	8.9
Yuban:						
Instant	6.7	3.3	2.3	2.5	0.9	8.2
Regular	2.1	1.1	0.7	0.5	0.1	5.1
Soluble Ratio	39.5	39.2	37.0	21.1	18.2	19.7

EXHIBIT 17

A Comparison of the Trend for Estimated Advertising Expenditures

Year	Total Coffee	20 Leading Grocery Product Manu-facturers	$ Coffee Expenditures
1958 = index	100	100	$43 million
1959	88	109	37
1960	117	109	50
1961	119	117	51
1962	106	120	45
1963	104	130	44

EXHIBIT 18

Research on Eight Product Descriptions for Freeze-Dried Coffee
(February 27, 1963)

Description	Percentage Rating As "One of Best" on Attributes					Would Buy (Percent)
	Flavor	Aroma	Strength	Quality	Freshness	
Extract of coffee	14	16	37	20	29	43
Freeze-dried coffee	17	16	17	19	49	48
Dry frozen coffee	10	7	25	17	46	52
Crystal coffee	14	14	6	21	40	45
Groundless coffee	12	13	21	21	38	45
Coffee concentrate	11	8	39	18	30	51
Whole coffee without grounds	26	27	30	26	42	52
Concentrated Crystals of Real Coffee	22	23	25	23	44	55

	Spontaneous Associations	
	Instant Coffee (Percent)	(Other)
Extract of coffee	22	(Flavoring agent, 19 percent)
Freeze-dried coffee	18	(Frozen, 32 percent)
Dry frozen coffee	17	(Frozen, 34 percent)
Crystal coffee	19	(Crystal clear, 47 percent)
Groundless coffee	29	(No sediment left in cup, 16 percent)
Coffee concentrate	42	(Stronger—won't need as much, 25 percent)
Whole coffee without grounds	41	(Whole coffee beans, 26 percent)
Concentrated Crystals of Real Coffee	44	(Grains/beads of coffee, 10 percent; Concentrated, 10 percent)

EXHIBIT 19

A Study of Four Candidate Names
(May, 1963)

Base: 463 respondents (women, "heads of households")

	MAXIM (Percent)	PRIMA (Percent)	NOVA (Percent)	KAABA (Control) (Percent)
Spontaneous Association				
With coffee	22	5	4	14
With Maxwell House	7	—	—	—
Spontaneous Association When Identified as Coffee				
Major association	Best/Maximum (37) Maxwell House (33)	High Quality (43)	New (24)	Foreign (45)
Not a suitable name	5	6	12	15
Anticipated Likes				
Will like nothing about it	12	13	25	32
Will dislike nothing about it	37	31	24	18
Expected Type				
Instant coffee	34	39	44	26
Regular coffee	51	35	22	34
New third type coffee	15	21	38	40
Rating Index by Characteristics (7 point scale: 4 = 100 index)				
Fresh	148	148	132	130
Fine aroma	135	132	112	118
Highest quality	135	135	110	112
Strong	132	115	100	130
Dark	125	110	102	132
Expensive	118	120	110	112
Modern	112	122	122	112
For men	106	90	90	112

EXHIBIT 20

Name Test—Choice of Gift Product from Three Alternatives*
(June, 1963)

					Percent of Users of				
	Total	Regular Ground	Instant	Both	Maxwell House	Regular Maxwell House	Instant Maxwell House	Both Maxwell House	Not Maxwell House
MAXIM	53	41	63	56	52	47	56	53	55
Nova	57	45	67	57	53	42	64	55	60
Maxwell House concentrated soluble	62	52	71	62	60	53	69	60	63
Maxwell House concentrated instant	62	48	73	64	59	47	73	55	64
Regular Maxwell House (average four tests)	28	50	4	29	28	50	5	29	28
Instant Maxwell House (average four tests)	14	3	27	8	16	3	24	15	12
Base: (average)	(300)	(100)	(100)	(100)	(150)	(56)	(56)	(38)	(150)

*In four matched tests the respondent was offered one of three products as a gift: namely, Regular Maxwell House, Instant Maxwell House, or one of the four descriptions for freeze-dried coffee. The table should be read as follows: Among all coffee drinkers (i.e., the total sample), who were given a choice of a description MAXIM versus IMH or RMH, 53 percent chose MAXIM, about 28 percent chose RMH and 14 percent chose IMH. Similarly if Nova was the description it was chosen 57 percent of the time over either IMH or RMH.

EXHIBIT 21

Telephone Study on the
Awareness, Association, and Connotations of "Soluble"
(April 6-7, 1963)

Association	Instant Coffee	Other	None Don't Know
Soluble coffee	36%	24%	40%
Concentrated soluble coffee	50	19	31
Soluble coffee concentrate	52	18	30

Awareness	Heard of Before	NOT Heard of Before
Soluble coffee	14%	86%
Concentrated soluble coffee	7	93
Soluble coffee concentrate	8	92

Definition (unaided)	Heard of Synonym	(Instant)	(Other)	Not Heard	Don't Know
Soluble coffee	16%	(14%)	(2%)	44%	(40%)
Concentrated soluble coffee	19	(18)	(1)	38	(43)
Soluble coffee concentrate	15	(15)	—	43	(42)

Definition (aided)	Regular Ground	Instant	Neither— 3rd Type
Soluble coffee	34%	37%	29%
Concentrated soluble coffee	20	53	27
Soluble coffee concentrate	2	61	37

Connotation	Better Than Instant	Same as Instant	Not as Good as Instant
Soluble coffee	7%	12%	10%
Concentrated soluble coffee	10	8	10
Soluble coffee concentrate	18	14	14

EXHIBIT 22

Test of Consumer Reaction to Maxim Square, Round, and Rectangular Jars
(January, 1964)

	Shown Square and Round		Shown Square and Rectangular	
	Square (Percent)	Round (Percent)	Square (Percent)	Rectangular (Percent)
Interest in Buying	59	58	55	64
Use instant only	62	70	62	78
Use only ground	40	38	40	40
Use both	72	66	64	74
Consider Different from Other Coffees	77	57	85	79
Faborable Product Evaluations				
Flavor	71	81	80	80
Aroma	69	79	82	84
Color	83	87	86	89
Strength	75	80	83	85
Overall quality	77	78	83	84
Improvement over other products	80	81	88	88
Favorable Packaging Evaluation				
Ease of handling	77	88	87	91
Ease of removing coffee	80	88	86	91
Ease of storage	82	86	92	94
Attractiveness	72	75	72	81
Cap style	87	90	88	88
Base: Female Heads of Households	(150)		(150)	

EXHIBIT 23

Male Influence in Coffee Brand Buying Decision Study (1962)

	Instant			Ground		
Household Coffee Usage	Total (Percent)	Use Instant Only (Percent)	Use Instant and Ground (Percent)	Total (Percent)	Use Ground Only (Percent)	Use Ground and Instant (Percent)
Husband asked directly for a brand, and wife bought it	18	18	18	16	15	17
(Wife did not buy it)	(1)	(—)*	(1)	(—)	(—)	(1)
Husband mentioned a brand, and wife bought it	8	5	8	9	7	10
Husband indicated dissatisfaction, and wife bought another brand	15	14	16	20	17	22
Husband bought a different brand	7	8	7	7	6	8
Husband shopped with wife and suggested a different brand, and wife bought it	8	10	8	9	8	10
(Wife did not buy it)	(—)	(—)	(—)	(1)	(2)	(—)
Husband did none of the above	65%	66%	65%	61%	61%	61%
Base: Total housewives in each group (no male interviews)	(753)	(96)	(657)	(200)	(88)	(112)

*Less than 0.05 percent.

EXHIBIT 24

Soluble Coffee Brand Expenditures on Media Advertising (Estimated 1963)

Total Dollars—By Region	Total	East	Mid-East	Central	West	South	West Central
IMH	$6,490	$1,710	$1,153	$1,048	$821	$1,053	$705
Nescafé	4,673	1,286	829	748	673	669	468
Sanka	2,981	675	448	462	520	464	412
Chase & Sanborn	3,243	946	582	574	267	611	263
Folger's	1,627	—	143	192	732	194	366
Yuban	2,440	1,221	433	255	352	162	17
Dollars per Thousand Population—By Region							
IMH	$34.33	$40.83	$43.09	$34.01	$25.63	$32.26	$28.29
Nescafé	24.72	30.71	30.98	24.28	21.01	20.49	18.78
Sanka	15.77	16.12	16.74	14.99	16.24	14.21	16.53
Chase & Sanborn	17.16	22.59	21.75	18.63	8.34	18.72	10.55
Folger's	8.61	—	5.34	6.23	22.85	5.94	14.69
Yuban	12.91	29.16	16.18	8.28	10.99	4.96	.68
1/1/64 Population (000).	189,039.3	41,878.6	26,755.1	30,813.4	32,028.3	32,645.2	24,918.7

EXHIBIT 25

**Comparative Projected National Costs of Alternative
Promotional Techniques**

	Cost Per Thousand	Extension
2-Ounce Jar and 25-Cent Coupon		
(Base: 25,000,000 homes)		
Product and package	$241.00	$ 6,025,000
Distribution	120.00	3,000,000
Carrier	13.00	325,000
Freeze-dry leaflets	6.00	150,000
25-cent coupon	5.00	125,000
Coupon redemption (25 percent)	67.50	1,687,500
Scoop	10.00	250,000
Transportation	6.00	150,000
Warehousing	5.00	125,000
	$473.50	$11,837,500
Free Coupon		
(Base: 9,000,000 homes)		
Coupon	$ 6.00	$ 54,000
Freeze-dry leaflets	6.00	54,000
Distribution	10.50	94,500
Postage	27.50	247,500
Coupon redemption (50 percent)	315.00	2,835,000
	$365.00	$ 3,285,000
6 Single Serving Packets and a 25-Cent Coupon		
(Base: 34,000,000 homes)		
Product	$130.50	$ 4,437,000
Container and top	4.50	153,000
Package	26.50	901,000
Handling	25.00	850,000
Postage	39.00	1,326,000
Leaflets	6.00	204,000
25-cent coupon	5.00	170,000
Redemption (25 percent)	67.50	2,295,000
Mailing carton	10.00	340,000
	$314.00	$10,676,000

EXHIBIT 26

Pricing Alternatives—Maxim

Brand	Size	Retail Price	Retail Price per Ounce	Retail Economy vs. Next Smaller Size	Cost* per Cup	Maxim per Ounce Premium
Maxim	2-oz.	$0.55	$0.2750	— %	2.12¢	— %
	4-oz.	0.85	0.2125	29.4	1.63	—
	8-oz.	1.59	0.1988	6.9	1.53	—
IMH	2-oz.	0.49	0.2450	—	1.88	12.2
	6-oz.	0.99	0.1650	48.5	1.27	28.8
	10-oz.	1.39†	0.1390	18.7	1.07	43.0
	14-oz.	1.89†	0.1350	3.0	1.04	47.3
IY	2-oz.	0.53	0.2650	—	2.04	3.8
	5-oz.	0.99	0.1980	33.8	1.52	7.3
	9-oz.	1.39†	0.1544	28.2	1.19	28.8
IS	2-oz,	0.53	0.2650	—	2.04	3.8
	5-oz.	1.09	0.2180	21.6	1.68	(7.5) .
	8-oz.	1.49†	0.1862	17.1	1.43	6.8
RMH	1-lb.	0.87	—	—	1.74	(2.3) A
	2-lb.	1.71	—	—	1.71	(7.0) B

*Soluble——13 cups per ounce. (A) versus 4-ounce.
Ground——50 cups per pound. (B) versus 8-ounce.
†Reflects retail shelf price when label packs of the following values are in distribution:

IMH	10-ounce	20 cents
IMH	14-ounce	30 cents
IY	9-ounce	20 cents
IS	8-ounce	10 cents

EXHIBIT 27

Pricing Alternatives—Maxim

Brand	Size	Retail Price	Retail Price per Ounce	Retail Economy vs. Next Smaller Size	Cost* per Cup	Maxim per Ounce Premium
Maxim	2-oz.	$0.57	$0.2850	— %	2.19¢	— %
	4-oz.	0.99	0.2475	15.1	1.90	—
	8-oz,	1.69	0.2112	17.2	1.63	—
IMH	2-oz.	0.49	0.2450	—	1.88	16.3
	6-oz.	0.99	0.1650	48.5	1.27	50.0
	10-oz.	1.39†	0.1390	18.7	1.07	51.9
	14-oz.	1.89†	0.1350	3.0	1.04	56.4
IY	2-oz.	0.53	0.1650	—	2.04	7.5
	5-oz.	0.99	0.1980	33.8	1.52	25.0
	9-oz.	1.39†	0.1544	12.8	1.19	36.8
IS	2-oz.	0.53	0.2650	—	2.04	7.5
	5-oz.	1.09	0.2180	21.6	1.68	13.5
	8-oz.	1.49†	0.1862	17.1	1.43	13.4
RMH	1-lb.	0.87	—	—	1.74	13.8 A
	2-lb.	1.71	—	—	1.71	4.7 B

*Soluble——13 cups per ounce (A) versus 4-ounce
Ground——50 cups per pound (B) versus 8-ounce
†Reflects retail shelf price when label packs of the following values are in distribution:

IMH	10-ounce	20 cents
IMH	14-ounce	30 cents
IY	9-ounce	20 cents
IS	8-ounce	10 cents

GENERAL FOODS CORPORATION-MAXIM [31]

MAXIMA[1] NEW PRODUCT PLANNING PROGRAM

MAXIMA is a computer program designed to help the marketing decision maker analyze the profit potential of a number of alternative new product marketing programs. It is an aid to decision-making since it minimizes the effort involved in comparing these alternatives according to their net present value. However, it is *not* a substitute for thinking, as there is no provision for checking the logic and consistency of each proposed plan.

The program is in two parts. The first section uses a simple 3-equation model (the Ayer model[32]) to predict the first year market share as a function of marketing mix. The second section uses this, plus cost data, to prepare profit-and-loss and cash-flow statements. There are also three optional "sub-models" which amplify some parts of the original program. These sub-models help to make it easier for the user to perform sensitivity analyses for the effects of growth, competition, and cannibalization and to mix different forms of promotion.

In the following sections, you will find a description of the model and operating instructions.

Ayer Model

The Ayer Model proper consists of two equations. The first predicts the percentage of the population who will be "aware" of the product at the end of a 13-week period. The second equation predicts the percentage who will make an "initial purchase" of the product.

These two equations are extended by a third one to give the market share at the end of the first year:

$$S = 1.05 * IP * \left[1 + e^{.35375* P-3.9486}\right]^{-1}$$

where IP is the percentage of initial purchasers, and P is the price per unit.

The third equation is justified as follows:

1. The trial rate at the end of the first year may be expected to be about 150% of that at the end of 13 weeks.

2. The first repeat rate is between 45 and 55% of the annual trial rate. This rate is a logarithmic function of retail price (from a high of $11.73 to a low of $10.60 for a unit of Maxim), i.e.

$$R = \left[1 + e^{-(B+C*P)}\right]^{-1}$$

   where B and C are constants

   $$B = 3.9486$$

   $$C = -0.35375$$

3. 70% of these repeat-buyers will become hard-core buyers.

---

[31] These materials were prepared by Henry J. Claycamp, George S. Day, and Charles B. Weinberg. S. Pocock and S. Springer assisted in the preparation and computer programming.

[32] A complete discussion of this model can be found in H. J. Claycamp and L. E. Liddy, "Prediction of New Product Performance: An Analytical Approach," *Journal of Marketing research,* November, 1969, pp. 414-420.

MAXIMA is a computer program designed to help the marketing decision maker analyze the profit potential of a number of alternative new product marketing programs. It is a decision-making aid that compares alternatives based on net present value. The program is in two parts. The first section uses a simple 3-equation model (the Ayer model, discussed in H. J. Claycamp and L. E. Liddy, "Prediction of New Product Performance: An Analytical Approach," Journal of Marketing Research, November 1969) to predict the first year market share as a function of marketing mix. The second section uses this, plus cost data, to prepare profit-and-loss and cash-flow statements. Sub-models help to perform sensitivity analysis on the marketing programs.

Promotion Blender

The three alternative promotions suggested in the case are not mutually exclusive. Number 1 covers the 25 million households in large cities; number 2 the 9 million in small cities and number 3 covers all 34 million households in the target population. Where the promotions cover different segments of the population, it would seem reasonable to combine their effects linearly in the Ayer Model.

This is the manipulation performed by the Promotion Blender. For example, taking 100% of number 1 and 100% of number 2 will give coverage of all 34 million households, as will 136% of number 1. Similarly, 74% of number 3 will reduce its coverage to just the large cities. If one feels that it is optimistic to sum the effects of the promotions, a Reduction Factor (say 10%) can be inserted.

It is stated in the case that number 1 extended to the entire target population costs the same per household. Thus the model calculates the cost of the combined promotion using a linear combination of costs (without Reduction factor).

Growth and Competition

The original model does not recognize competition. Although it is not possible to predict what competition *will* do, the Growth and Competition model is intended to make it easier to perform sensitivity analyses on the likely effect of competition.

We assume that there is a "market" for freeze-dried coffee. This market will grow under the influence of advertising by Maxwell House and its competitors. Thus, if the first-year market is X, we can say that the market in any year will be XZ, where Z is a growth factor "with competition."

This market for freeze-dried coffee will be divided between the companies operating in it. We assume this split to be proportional to what the companies would have achieved individually. We have calculated that Maxwell House alone would have achieved X in the first year: say that competition would have achieved Y. Then we assume that Maxwell House's share of the freeze-dried market will be

$$\frac{X}{X + Y}$$

We can derive Y by estimating a "competitive effectiveness," V, relative to Maxwell House. Then $Y = VX$ and:

$$\text{Maxwell House market} = X*Z*(\frac{1}{1 + V})$$

In this sub-model, we further assume that the market share derived from the Ayer Model refers to the home market. We add on a bit to cover the freeze-dried share of the commercial market. Calculations suggested that 11.3% of the coffee market was "commercial"—used in restaurants etc.—and it was estimated that 0.28 of this might be taken by freeze dried coffee. These numbers are already entered as data in the program, but they can easily be changed. Since other people may get different values, depending on what they assume included in "Total Market," the user is advised to check the calculation and change the data if it is significantly wrong.

Note that the sub-model requires a growth factor for year 1. Presumably, if competition entered the market at the same time as Maxwell House, this factor would be greater than zero because of the extra promotion.

Cannibalization Model

The first part of the model tries to determine how many units of the freeze-dried market are attributable to Maxwell House; the second part allows sensitivity analyses on the loss likely to be suffered by Maxwell House.

It would seem wrong to blame the entire freeze-dried market on to Maxim. Even if Maxwell House stays out of the market, competition will probably enter. Thus only the incremental market caused by the Maxim decision should be debited to Maxim's profitability.

If, as before, we assume that Maxim would achieve a market of X; and competition one of Y, in year 1; and if we assume that in any year, the market growth with Maxim is Z; and for competition alone it would have been G, then the incremental market due to Maxim is:

$$XZ - YG$$

And if we assume that $Y = XV$, as before, then the incremental loss reduces to

$$X*(Z - V*G)$$

The simplest assumption is that this loss is borne by all brands in proportion to their market share. This is the basis of the second part of the sub-model: but it is possible to perform sensitivity analyses on the effect of tipping the balance to or from Maxwell House, or between regular and instant.

1. "% from Maxwell House" reduces the impact of cannibalization by the percentage specified. (A negative figure increases the impact.)

2. "% from Instant" transfers this percentage of the cannibalized *Instant Volume* to regular. If the percentage is negative, this percentage of the Regular Volume is moved to Instant. (So that the volume transferred by +10% is different to that for −10%.)

At this stage one can also specify how much of the $0.7 per unit advertising expanded on the cannibalized units is cut. 100% Adcut means that it is all stopped: 0% means that advertising continues as before.

Note that as the sub-model is set up at present, an advertising cut is taken only on the volumes cannibalized by Maxim. It is implied that there will be no reduction on the volumes of business lost to competitive freeze-dried coffees.

Profit Model

The profit model proceeds through the stages of calculating annual sales, plant cost, profit-and-loss statements, cash-flow calculations, pay-back year and net-present-value. All printout can be suppressed except the plant-cost, pay-back year and net-present-value.

Annual Sales. The user specifies the anticipated total market (in units), and growth factors for the second and third years. Beyond this time it is assumed that freeze-dried coffee has a stable share of the market, and that this grows at 3% per year in line with the total market.

Plant Cost. Plant is assumed to cost $5 per unit of capacity (as specified in the case). The model assumes building plant to meet the *average* expected demand over the years of stable growth (years 4 to the horizon year, inclusive). For profit-and-loss and tax purposes, straight-line depreciation is used.

Profit-and-Loss Statements. If required, these are calculated for the first three years. Marketing costs comprise the advertising costs for the three years and the promotion costs for the first year, as input by the user. There is a trade promotion of $3.5 million in the first year and $2.0 million in subsequent years. There are also direct sales expenses of $1.7 million in each year— Maxim's share of the total Maxwell House direct sales expenses.

The margin on each unit of coffee allows $5.72 variable cost as specified in the case, and 13% margin to the retailer.

To calculate the incremental contribution, it is necessary to allow for losses from cannibalization volumes of Regular and Instant. This may be reduced if the advertising and promotion budgets for these brands are reduced in proportion to the expected loss of volume. An estimate of these budgets is $0.70 per unit (total).

Cash Flow Calculations. These are calculated after tax. Marketing costs for the first three years are as calculated in the previous section. Beyond year 3, both they and cannibalization losses are assumed to increase at the rate of market growth. The tax rate is taken as 48%, and a credit is allowed for depreciation. The model assumes that the Maxwell House division as a whole is profitable, so that the tax credit for depreciation can be taken even when the Maxim project itself is making a loss.

Pay-back Year. This is automatically calculated and printed out so as to summarize one salient feature of the Cash-flow.

Net-Present-Value. The net-present-value (N.P.V.) of the project is calculated for the interest rate specified by the user. The internal rate of return is found by experiment (to get an N.P.V. of zero).

Operating the Program

The data requirements and the program outline are summarized in Exhibits 1–4, and the program listing and further notes can be found on pages 82–83.

At the beginning of each run, the user specifies which sub-models (if any) he requires for that run. Throughout the program, any request for input that is preceded and followed by an asterisk (e.g. * RE-RUN*?) expects a Yes/No answer—"Y" or "N" is sufficient.

The Ayer and Profit models can be run separately. Before the first run of each section, the program requests input of all the data for that section. Thereafter, if the user elects to re-run the program, he can change individual items of data. To do this, he specifies:

1. How many items he wishes to change

2. For each item
   a. the reference number of the variable
   b. the new value

Note: At this point, the user may change not only the variables he has input, but also some of the data pre-set in the program—namely, variables 35 to 43.

In the Profit Model, the tables of sales, profit-and-loss and cash flow are printed out only on request.

Before calculating the N.P.V., the program requests a Discount Rate. It then requests a new rate: *If this is entered at zero, the program stops calculating present values and moves to the next run.*

Exhibits 1 and 2 contain a list of variables and suggested values for some of the variables. It is worth contemplating what the model means: particularly, what is the "population" to which the percentages refer? A sample run is given in Exhibit 3.

If the user has forgotten the current values that he has assigned to the program variables, he types "LIST" (or "L") after the query * RE-RUN*? He then receives a listing of all the variables so far entered into the program (by reference number) with their values. A flow chart is included as Exhibit 4.

It is useful to list the entire data requirements down the side of a piece of paper, and to enter the values for each of the intended runs in columns: all the data in the first column, and the changes only in the subsequent ones.

All the cost data are entered in dollars: this is made much easier using the "E" notation. For example, 12,500,000 is entered as 125E5.

Unfortunately this program does not solve the case. It merely manipulates data. *It is therefore necessary to work out what one wants to run before going to the terminal.* In particular, there are a lot of interactions between the data— for example, market growth is probably associated with high advertising and promotion—but the user has to evaluate this. However, it is easy (and entirely acceptable) to modify any aspects of the model.

EXHIBIT 1

List of Variables

Variable Number	Variable Name	Notes
1	Media Impressions per Household	Number in 13 weeks: AHI
2	Percent of Households Available	CU
3	Family Brand	FB
4	Value of Promotion as Advertising	CP* } values suggested in Appendix
5	Value of Promotion as Promotion	CP }
6	% Market Share	Entered if Ayer Model not run
7	Price	per unit—somewhere between $9 and $12
8	Market Size	in units
9	Second year sales growth	Growth as a percentage of first-year sales
10	Third-year sales growth	Growth as a percentage of first-year sales
11	Horizon Year	maximum 20
12	Residual Value %	Value of plant as % of initial cost at the end of Horizon year ($)
13	Advertising Cost (Year 1)	In $
14	Advertising Cost (Year 2)	In $
15	Advertising Cost (Year 3)	In $
16	Promotion Cost (Year 1)	In $
17	Cannibalization (Year 1)	} Loss of contribution on other Maxwell House Coffees (in $ after any advertising reduction)
18	Cannibalization (Year 2)	}
19	Cannibalization (Year 3)	}
20	Percent of Promotion 1	
21	Percent of Promotion 2	
22	Percent of Promotion 3	
23	Reduction Factor	A percentage reduction in the values of CP & CP*

Discussion Assignment

1. Develop a national marketing plan for General Foods' new freeze-dried coffee. Be sure to fully specify your objectives and the assumptions underlying each component of your strategy. Describe the alternative strategies you considered and your reasons for rejecting them. Use the MAXIMA computer model to test the sales and profit implications of the alternative strategies.

2. Analyze the pros and cons of the alternatives of GO (national or regional introduction), NO-GO (stop development) or ON (test market) and make a recommendation for further action to top management. If test marketing is recommended, specify what is to be learned during the test.

Variable Number	Variable Name	Notes
24	Growth with competition (Year 1)	Percentage relative to the Ayer Model estimate of first-year market
25	Growth with competition (Year 2)	
26	Growth with competition (Year 3)	
27	Competitive effectiveness (Year 1)	Percentage relative to Maxwell House
28	Competitive effectiveness (Year 2)	
29	Competitive effectiveness (Year 3)	
30	Growth without Maxwell House (Year 2)	Percentage growth of the market that competition alone would have achieved, relative to Year 1.
31	Growth without Maxwell House (Year 3)	
32	Percent from Maxwell House	A percentage reduction in Maxwell House's share of the cannibalization losses
33	Percent from Instant	A percentage of the Instant losses from cannibalization (by volume) transferred to regular (A negative value transfer—percentage of the Regular volume to Instant)
34	Percent Advertising Cut	Percent reduction in the Advertising per unit on the volume cannibalized by Maxim
35	Product Positioning	PP: entered as 52
36	Copy execution	CE: entered as 64
37	Consumer Interest	CI: entered as 38
38	Retail Distribution	DN: entered as 70
39	Package Distinctiveness	PK: entered as 60
40	Consumer Satisfaction	PS*: entered as 80
41	Percentage of market that is "commercial"	Only in "Growth + Competition" submodel: entered as 11.3
42	Fraction of commercial market available to Freeze Dried Coffee	In "Growth + Competition" entered as 0.28
43	Market Growth	Stable growth of coffee market: entered as 1.03 (i.e. 3%)

EXHIBIT 2

Inputs to the Ayer Model

(A) Awareness of Advertising

$$AR = -35.88 + .76(PP) + 2.12 \sqrt{AHI \times CE} + .039(CP^*) + .392(CI)$$

(i) PP = Judged product positioning. This should be set at 52 in the program since it requires complex judgments about product benefits, and concept form and package uniqueness (where $\overline{PP}$ = 35.6 and σ = 15.3).

(ii) AHI = average number of media impressions *per household*. The following input values have been developed for the three alternative advertising programs:

Media Plan	Reach[33] (percent of target audience)	Frequency (number of times target audience exposed in 1st 13 weeks)	Annual Budget (Budget in first 13 weeks is 43% of this amount)	Total Number of Adjusted Household Impressions (during first 13 weeks)	AHI Per Household (during first 13 weeks)
1.	.85 urban households .55 other households	13	$12,800,000	540,000,000	9.63
2.	.85 urban households .55 other households	12	11,600,000	498,000,000	8.74
3.	.85 urban households .55 other households	10	9,500,000	415,000,000	7.28

[33]Based on an estimate of 34,000,000 urban households and 23,000,000 non-urban households, with incomes over $3500.

(iii) CE = copy execution

This is an assessment of execution, which encompasses the freshness and appropriateness of the advertisement, possibilities for brand identification effectiveness of demonstrations (if any), suitability of tone and language, and opportunities for involvement. Based upon an analysis of Appendix 1 of the case a reasonable input value is 6.40 (although $\overline{CE}$ = 7.30 and σ = 1.5).

(iv) CP* = value of promotion in advertising recall. This variable indicates the type and coverage of consumer promotion containing advertising messages for the product. The following input values have been based on an analysis of the three promotion plans described in Exhibit 30 of the case.

Plan		Cost $	Input Value
A	2-oz jar and 25¢ coupon (25,000,000 households)	11,873,500	108
B	Coupon for free 2-oz jar (9,000,000 households)	3,285,000	32
C	Six single serving packets (34,000,000 households)	10,676,000	135

(v) CI = index of consumer interest in the product category. This should be set at an average of 38 in the program (where $\overline{CI}$ = 37.5 and σ = 5.7).

(B) Initial Purchase (Trial) Rate

$$IP = -16.01 + .370(AR) + .194(DN \times PK) + 9.24(FB) + .09(CP) + .022(PS^*) + .067(CU)$$

(i) AR = predicted advertising awareness from previous equation

(ii) DN = percent of all commodity distribution that will probably be achieved after 13 weeks, weighted to account for shelf facings and displays. This should be set at 70 in this program (DN = 58.5 with σ = 14.8) to reflect the ability of General Foods to obtain distribution.

(iii) PK = the impact of the graphics, shape and subsequent usefulness of the package. This should be set at 60 in this program ($\overline{PK}$ = 55.6 with σ = 13.2).

(iv) FB = the family brand variable which is set at 0 if the brand is completely new to the market, 1.0 if it is an addition to a well known family of brands, or some value between 0 and 1.0 if there is a limited association between the new brand and an established brand name.

(v) CP = ability of promotional activities to induce trial (this has a different value than CP*) ($\overline{CP}$ = 63.9 and σ = 55.1). Judgments for the values of CP for the three promotional plans listed above are as follows:

Plan	Input Value
A	108
B	39
C	123

(vi) PS* = index of consumer satisfaction with new product samples. Set at an average value of 80 in the model ($\overline{PS^*}$ = 77.4 and σ = 45).

(vii) CU = percentage of households using products in the category. Set at an average value of 90 ($\overline{CU}$ = 67.0 and σ = 23.2).

EXHIBIT 3

Sample Runs of MAXIMA

```
RUN
FMXMA

SUB-MØDELS:  DØ YØU REQUIRE(YES ØR NØ)  -
             *PRØMØTIØN BLENDER*?N
             *GRØWTH + CØMPETITIØN*?N
             *CANNIBALISATIØN MØDEL*?N

*AYER MØDEL*?Y

MEDIA IMPRSSNS PER HSHLD, %HSHLD AVAIL?9.63,90
NEW BRAND ØR ØNE ØF FAMILY (0 TØ 1)?1
PRICE?11
VAL ØF PRØMØTIØN: AS ADVTSG, AS PRØM?108,108

             AWARENESS % = 39.203
             INITIAL PCHSRS %= 32.9651
             MKT SHARE %= 17.8028

*PRØFIT MØDEL*?Y

MKT SIZE?60E6
SALES GRØWTH: % YR2, YR3?20,40
HØRIZØN YR. PLANT RESID VAL %?5,50
AD-CØST: YRS 1, 2, 3?12.8E6,6.4E6,6.4E6
PRØM-CØST:  YR 1?11.9E6
CANNIBALISATIØN: YR 1,2,3?6E6,6E6,7E6

*SALES*?Y

YEARLY SALES (IN UNITS)

YEAR          SALES

1             1.06817E+07
2             1.28180E+07
3             1.49544E+07
4             1.54030E+07
5             1.58651E+07

*P+L*?Y

PRØFIT AND LØSS STATEMENT IN THØUSANDS ØF DØLLARS

                     YEAR 1        YEAR 2        YEAR 3

SALES                117499.       140998.       164498.
GRØSS MARGIN         41124.        49349.        57574.

MARKETING CØSTS      29900         10100         10100
DEPRECIATIØN         7704          7704          7704

GRØSS CØNTRIBUTIØN   3520          31545         39770.

CANNIBALISATIØN      6000          6000          7000

INCREMENTAL PRØFIT   -2480         25545         32770.

*CASH FLØW*?Y

ANNUAL SALES AND AFTER-TAX CASH FLØW

YEAR       SALES (UNITS)  CASH FLØW

0          0              -7.70374E+07
1          1.06817E+07    6.41453E+06
2          1.28180E+07    2.09875E+07
3          1.49544E+07    2.47444E+07
4          1.54030E+07    2.53758E+07
5          1.58651E+07    6.45449E+07
```

Cash flow in last year includes residual value of plant.

```
PLANT CØST = $ 7.70374E+07
PAYBACK YR 4

DISCØUNT RATE %?8
NET PRESENT VALUE =$ 2.91185E+07

NEW DISCØUNT RATE %?17
NET PRESENT VALUE =$ 2.20788E+06

NEW DISCØUNT RATE %?19
NET PRESENT VALUE =$-2.44106E+06

NEW DISCØUNT RATE %?18.5
NET PRESENT VALUE =$-1.31594E+06

NEW DISCØUNT RATE %?0

*RE-RUN*?N

DØNE
```

Exhibit 3 (cont.)

```
RUN
FMXMA

SUB-MØDELS:  DØ YØU REQUIRE(YES ØR NØ)  -
             *PRØMØTIØN BLENDER*?Y
             *GRØWTH + CØMPETITIØN*?Y
             *CANNIBALISATIØN MØDEL*?Y


*AYER MØDEL*?Y

MEDIA IMPRSSNS PER HSHLD, %HSHLD AVAIL?9.63,90
NEW BRAND ØR ØNE ØF FAMILY (0 TØ 1)?.7
PRICE?11
PRØM MIX: %1, %2, %3,REDN FACTØR?0,0,100,0

             PRØMØTIØN CØST = $MN 10.68
             AWARENESS % = 40.2685
             INITIAL PCHSRS %= 31.8758
             MKT SHARE %= 17.2145

*PRØFIT MØDEL*?Y

MKT SIZE?60E6
GRØWTH WITH CØMPETN:% YR1, YR2, YR3?0,20,50
CØMPET EFFECTIVENESS:% YR1, YR2, YR3?0,30,80
HØRIZØN YR. PLANT RESID VAL %?5,50
AD-CØST: YRS 1, 2, 3?12.8E6,6.4E6,6.4E6
PRØM-CØST: YR 1?10.7E6
MKT GRØWTH (NØ MAXWELL HØUSE): % YR2, YR3?10,20
% FRØM MAXWELL HØUSE, % FRØM INSTANT?0,10
% ADVERTISING CUT?20

*SALES*?N
*P+L*?N
*CASH FLØW*?N

PLANT CØST = $ 4.74796E+07
PAYBACK YR 5

DISCØUNT RATE %?12
NET PRESENT VALUE =$ 8.48863E+06

NEW DISCØUNT RATE %?0

*RE-RUN*?Y


HØW MANY DATA ITEMS DØ YØU WISH TØ CHANGE?3

INPUT: NØ. ØF VARIABLE, NEW VALUE (ØNE PAIR PER LINE)
?20,100
?22,0
?16,11.8E6

*AYER MØDEL*?Y

             PRØMØTIØN CØST = $MN 11.87
             AWARENESS % = 39.2155
             INITIAL PCHSRS %= 30.1962
             MKT SHARE %= 16.3075

*PRØFIT MØDEL*?Y

*SALES*?N
*P+L*?N
*CASH FLØW*?N

PLANT CØST = $ 4.54072E+07
PAYBACK YR 5

DISCØUNT RATE %?12
NET PRESENT VALUE =$ 6.39183E+06

NEW DISCØUNT RATE %?0

*RE-RUN*?L


VARIABLE NUMBERS AND VALUES

    1       9.63
    2       90
    3       .7
    6       16.3075
    7       11
    8       6.00000E+07
   11       5
   12       50
   13       1.28000E+07
   14       6.40000E+06
   15       6.40000E+06
   16       1.18000E+07
   20       100
   21       0
```

Exhibit 3 (cont.)

```
22    0
23    0
24    0
25    20
26    50
27    0
28    30
29    80
30    10
31    20
32    0
33    10
34    20
35    52
36    6.4
37    38
38    70
39    .6
40    80
41    11.3
42    .28
43    1.03
```

∗ RE-RUN∗?N

EXHIBIT 4

MAXIMA Program Outline

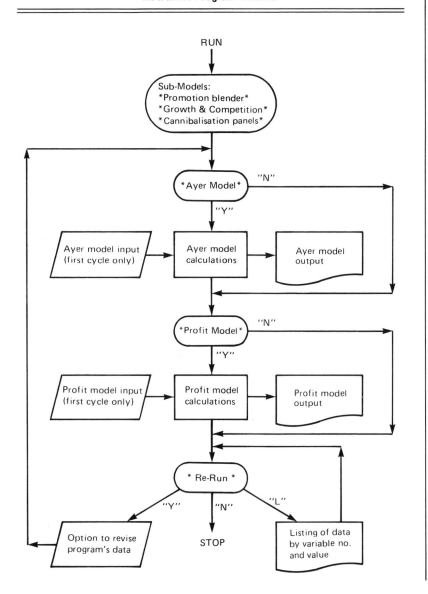

Exhibit 4 (cont.)

AYER MODEL CALCULATIONS

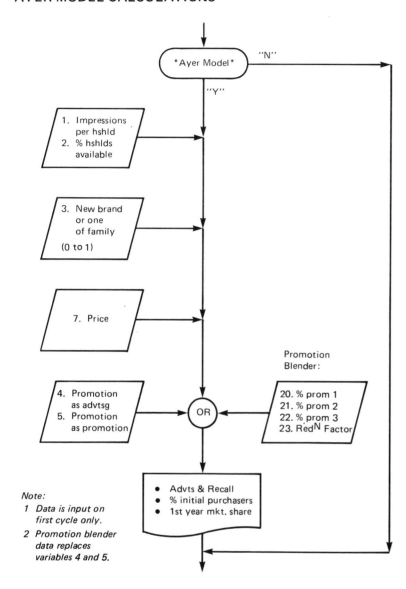

Note:
1 Data is input on
first cycle only.

2 Promotion blender
data replaces
variables 4 and 5.

Exhibit 4 (cont.)

PROFIT MODEL CALCULATIONS

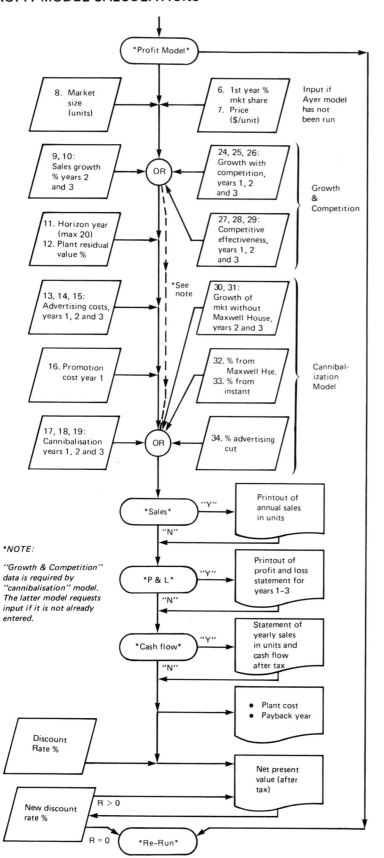

MAXIMA PROGRAM LISTING

MAXIMA—A Few Words About The Program

All the variables input by the user are assigned an element of the vector X, as are 8 items of data written into the program. There are 43 elements in X, and they can all be altered by the data-change option. Their reference numbers are as listed in the main write-up.

There are additionally a number of variables calculated by the program. They are as follows:

Ayer Model:	A	Advertising Recall
	I	% Initial purchasers
	S(N)	Unit sales in year N
	N = 1 to 20	
Profit Model:	K	Plant cost
	T	Total sales in units (year 3—horizon)
	D	Annual depreciation
	M1	Unit margin in $
	L(N)	Dollar sales ⎫
	M(N)	Gross margin ⎪ first
	E(N)	Marketing expense ⎬ 3
	G(N)	Gross contribution ⎪ years
	C(N)	Incremental contribution ⎭
	N = 1 to 3	
	F(N)	Annual cash-flow
	N = 1 to 20	
	B	Cumulative cash-flow for payback
	V	Net present value
	R	Discount rate
Promotion Blender:	P	Cost of promotion
Growth & Competition:	S2	% share of total market
Cannibalization Model:	U(N)	Units cannibalized in total and due to Maxwell House
	N = 1 to 3	
	W1	Dollar cost to Instant for each unit cannibalized
	W2	Dollar cost to Regular for each unit cannibalized
	T9	Total cost to Maxwell House for each unit cannibalized
Other variables:	P$	Promotion Blender
	G$	Growth & Competition
	C$	Cannibalization
	N$	All other Yes/No answers
	Z1	Control of data input, Ayer Model
	Z2	Control of data input, project model
	J	No. of data items to be charged
	Y1	Response number of changed variable
	Y2	New value of changed variable
	I	Control variable for all cycles in program

MAXIMA PROGRAM LISTING

MXMA

```
20    REM PRØGRAM PREPARED AT STANFØRD UNIVERSITY
30    LET Z1=Z2=0
40    DIM X[45],S[20],M[3],E[3],G[3],C[3],F[20],U[3],L[3]
50    DIM P$[4],G$[4],C$[4],N$[4]
60    READ X[35],X[36],X[37],X[38],X[39],X[40],X[41],X[42],X[43]
70    DATA 52,6.4,38,70,.6,80,11.3,.28,1.03
80    PRINT "SUB-MØDELS:   DØ YØU REQUIRE(YES ØR NØ)   -"
90    PRINT TAB(12)"*PRØMØTIØN BLENDER*";
100   INPUT P$
110   PRINT TAB(12)"*GRØWTH + CØMPETITIØN*";
120   INPUT G$
130   PRINT TAB(12)"*CANNIBALISATIØN MØDEL*";
140   INPUT C$
150   PRINT
160   PRINT
170   PRINT
180   PRINT "*AYER MØDEL*";
190   INPUT N$
200   IF N$[1,1]="Y" THEN 500
210   PRINT
220   PRINT "*PRØFIT MØDEL*";
230   INPUT N$
240   PRINT
250   IF N$[1,1] <> "Y" THEN 3640
270   IF Z2=1 THEN 310
280   PRINT "1ST YR % MKT SHARE, PRICE";
290   INPUT X[6],X[7]
310   GØTØ 1000
500   REM AYER MØDEL
510   IF Z1=1 THEN 590
520   PRINT
530   PRINT "MEDIA IMPRSSNS PER HSHLD, %HSHLD AVAIL";
540   INPUT X[1],X[2]
550   PRINT "NEW BRAND ØR ØNE ØF FAMILY (0 TØ 1)";
560   INPUT X[3]
570   PRINT "PRICE";
580   INPUT X[7]
590   IF P$[1,1]="Y" THEN 5000
600   IF Z1=1 THEN 630
610   PRINT "VAL ØF PRØMØTIØN: AS ADVTSG, AS PRØM";
620   INPUT X[4],X[5]
630   PRINT
640   LET A=-35.876+.756*X[35]+2.122*SQR(X[1]*X[36])+.039*X[4]+.392*X[37]
650   LET I=-16.011+.37*A+.194*X[38]*X[39]+9.245*X[3]+.086*X[5]+.022*X[40]
660   LET X[6]=1.05*I/(1+EXP(.35375*X[7]-3.9486))
670   PRINT TAB(12)"AWARENESS % =";A
680   PRINT TAB(12)"INITIAL PCHSRS %=";I
690   PRINT TAB(12)"MKT SHARE %=";X[6]
700   PRINT
710   LET Z1=1
720   PRINT "*PRØFIT MØDEL*";
730   INPUT N$
740   PRINT
750   IF N$[1,1] <> "Y" THEN 3640
1000  REM PRØFIT MØDEL
1010  REM DATA INPUT
1020  IF Z2=1 THEN 1050
1030  PRINT "MKT SIZE";
1040  INPUT X[8]
1050  IF G$[1,1]="Y" THEN 5500
1060  IF Z2=1 THEN 1090
1070  PRINT "SALES GRØWTH: % YR2, YR3";
1080  INPUT X[9],X[10]
1090  LET S[1]=X[8]*X[6]/100
1100  LET S[2]=S[1]*(100+X[9])/100
1110  LET S[3]=S[1]*(100+X[10])/100
1120  IF Z2=1 THEN 1190
1130  PRINT "HØRIZØN YR. PLANT RESID VAL %";
1140  INPUT X[11],X[12]
1150  PRINT "AD-CØST: YRS 1, 2, 3";
1160  INPUT X[13],X[14],X[15]
1170  PRINT "PRØM-CØST:  YR 1";
1180  INPUT X[16]
1190  IF C$[1,1]="Y" THEN 6000
1200  IF Z2=1 THEN 1500
1210  PRINT "CANNIBALISATIØN: YR 1,2,3";
1220  INPUT X[17],X[18],X[19]
1230  PRINT
1500  REM SALES CALCULATIØNS
1510  FØR I=4 TØ X[11]
1520  LET S[I]=S[I-1]*X[43]
1530  NEXT I
1540  PRINT "*SALES*";
1550  INPUT N$
1560  IF N$[1,1] <> "Y" THEN 2000
1570  PRINT
1580  PRINT "YEARLY SALES (IN UNITS)"
1585  PRINT
1590  PRINT "YEAR","SALES"
1600  PRINT
1610  FØR I=1 TØ X[11]
1620  PRINT I,S[I]
```

```
1630  NEXT I
1640  PRINT
1650  PRINT
2000  REM PLANT CØST
2010  LET T=0
2020  FØR I=3 TØ X[11]
2030  LET T=T+S[I]
2040  NEXT I
2050  LET K=5*T/(X[11]-2)
2060  REM PLANT CØST PRINTED JUST BEFØRE PAYBACK YR
2080  LET D=K*(100-X[12])/(100*X[11])
2500  REM PRØFIT + LØSS
2510  LET M1=X[7]*.87-5.72
2520  LET E[1]=X[13]+X[16]+3.5E+06+1.7E+06
2530  LET E[2]=X[14]+2.E+06+1.7E+06
2540  LET E[3]=X[15]+2.E+06+1.7E+06
2550  PRINT "*P+L*";
2560  INPUT N$
2580  IF N$[1,1] <> "Y" THEN 3000
2590  FØR I=1 TØ 3
2600  LET L[I]=INT(X[7]*S[I]/1000+.5)
2610  LET M[I]=INT(M1*S[I]/1000+.5)
2620  LET G[I]=INT(M[I]-(E[I]+D)/1000+.5)
2630  LET C[I]=INT(G[I]-X[16+I]/1000+.5)
2640  NEXT I
2650  PRINT
2660  PRINT "PRØFIT AND LØSS STATEMENT IN THØUSANDS ØF DØLLARS"
2670  PRINT
2680  PRINT TAB(21)"YEAR 1";TAB(36)"YEAR 2";TAB(51)"YEAR 3"
2690  PRINT
2700  PRINT "SALES";TAB(20);L[1];TAB(35);L[2];TAB(50);L[3]
2710  PRINT "GRØSS MARGIN";TAB(20);M[1];TAB(35);M[2];TAB(50);M[3]
2720  PRINT
2730  PRINT "MARKETING CØSTS";TAB(20);INT(E[1]/1000+.5);
2731  PRINT TAB(35);INT(E[2]/1000+.5);TAB(50);INT(E[3]/1000+.5)
2740  PRINT "DEPRECIATIØN";TAB(20);INT(D/1000+.5);
2741  PRINT TAB(35);INT(D/1000+.5);TAB(50);INT(D/1000+.5)
2750  PRINT
2760  PRINT "GRØSS CØNTRIBUTIØN ";TAB(20);G[1];TAB(35);G[2];TAB(50);G[3]
2770  PRINT
2780  PRINT "CANNIBALISATIØN";TAB(20);INT(X[17]/1000+.5);
2781  PRINT TAB(35);INT(X[18]/1000+.5);TAB(50);INT(X[19]/1000+.5)
2790  PRINT
2800  PRINT "INCREMENTAL PRØFIT";TAB(20);C[1];TAB(35);C[2];TAB(50);C[3]
2810  PRINT
2820  PRINT
3000  REM CASH FLØW CALCULATIØN
3010  FØR I=1 TØ 3
3020  LET F[I]=(M1*S[I]-E[I]-X[16+I])*.52+.48*D
3030  NEXT I
3040  FØR I=3 TØ X[11]
3050  LET F[I]=(M1*S[I]-(E[3]+X[19])*X[43]+(I-3))*.52+.48*D
3060  NEXT I
3070  LET F[X[11]]=F[X[11]]+X[12]*K/100
3080  PRINT "*CASH FLØW*";
3090  INPUT N$
3100  IF N$[1,1] <> "Y" THEN 3210
3110  PRINT
3120  PRINT "ANNUAL SALES AND AFTER-TAX CASH FLØW"
3130  PRINT
3140  PRINT "YEAR","SALES (UNITS)","CASH FLØW"
3150  PRINT
3160  PRINT 0,0,-K
3170  FØR I=1 TØ X[11]
3180  PRINT I,S[I],F[I]
3190  NEXT I
3200  PRINT
3210  PRINT
3220  REM PAYBACK YEAR + PLANT CØST PRINTØUT
3225  PRINT "PLANT CØST = $";K
3230  LET B=-K
3240  FØR I=1 TØ X[11]
3250  LET B=B+F[I]
3260  IF B >= 0 THEN 3300
3270  NEXT I
3280  PRINT "PAYBACK BEYØND YR";X[11]
3290  GØTØ 3310
3300  PRINT "PAYBACK YR";I
3310  PRINT
3500  REM NPV CALCULATIØN
3510  PRINT "DISCØUNT RATE %";
3520  INPUT R
3530  LET V=-K
3540  FØR I=1 TØ X[11]
3550  LET V=V+F[I]/((1+R/100)+I)
3560  NEXT I
3570  PRINT "NET PRESENT VALUE =$";V
3580  PRINT
3590  PRINT "NEW DISCØUNT RATE %";
3600  INPUT R
3620  IF R <> 0 THEN 3530
3630  LET Z2=1
3640  PRINT
3650  PRINT "*RE-RUN*";
3660  INPUT N$
3670  PRINT
3680  PRINT
```

```
3690    IF N$[1,1]="L" THEN 4500
3700    IF N$[1,1] <> "Y" THEN 9999
4000    REM INPUT NEW DATA
4010    PRINT "HØW MANY DATA ITEMS DØ YØU WISH TØ CHANGE";
4020    INPUT J
4030    IF J=0 THEN 4100
4040    PRINT
4050    PRINT "INPUT: NØ. ØF VARIABLE, NEW VALUE (ØNE PAIR PER LINE)"
4060    FØR I=1 TØ J
4070    INPUT Y1,Y2
4080    LET X[Y1]=Y2
4090    NEXT I
4100    GØTØ 160
4500    REM LIST-ØUT ØF VARIABLES
4510    PRINT "VARIABLE NUMBERS AND VALUES"
4520    PRINT
4530    IF Z1=0 THEN 4910
4540    FØR I=1 TØ 3
4550    PRINT I;X[I]
4560    NEXT I
4570    IF P$[1,1]="Y" THEN 4600
4580    PRINT 4;X[4]
4590    PRINT 5;X[5]
4600    PRINT 6;X[6]
4605    PRINT 7;X[7]
4610    IF Z2=0 THEN 4725
4620    PRINT 8;X[8]
4630    IF G$[1,1]="Y" THEN 4660
4640    PRINT 9;X[9]
4650    PRINT 10;X[10]
4660    FØR I=11 TØ 16
4670    PRINT I;X[I]
4680    NEXT I
4690    IF C$[1,1]="Y" THEN 4725
4700    FØR I=17 TØ 19
4710    PRINT I;X[I]
4720    NEXT I
4725    IF Z1=0 THEN 4765
4730    IF P$[1,1] <> "Y" THEN 4765
4740    FØR I=20 TØ 23
4750    PRINT I;X[I]
4760    NEXT I
4765    IF Z2=0 THEN 4860
4770    IF G$[1,1]="Y" THEN 4790
4780    IF C$[1,1] <> "Y" THEN 4820
4790    FØR I=24 TØ 29
4800    PRINT I;X[I]
4810    NEXT I
4820    IF C$[1,1] <> "Y" THEN 4860
4830    FØR I=30 TØ 34
4840    PRINT I;X[I]
4850    NEXT I
4860    FØR I=35 TØ 43
4870    PRINT I;X[I]
4880    NEXT I
4890    PRINT
4900    GØTØ 3640
4910    IF Z2=0 THEN 4860
4920    GØTØ 4600
5000    REM PRØMØTIØN BLENDER
5010    IF Z1=1 THEN 5040
5020    PRINT "PRØM MIX: %1, %2, %3,REDN FACTØR";
5030    INPUT X[20],X[21],X[22],X[23]
5040    LET X[4]=(108*X[20]+32*X[21]+135*X[22])/(100+X[23])
5050    LET X[5]=(108*X[20]+39*X[21]+123*X[22])/(100+X[23])
5060    LET P=.1187*X[20]+.0329*X[21]+.1068*X[22]
5070    PRINT
5080    PRINT TAB(12)"PRØMØTIØN CØST = $MN";P
5090    GØTØ 640
5500    REM GRØWTH + CØMPETITIØN
5510    IF Z2=1 THEN 5560
5520    PRINT "GRØWTH WITH CØMPETN:% YR1, YR2, YR3";
5530    INPUT X[24],X[25],X[26]
5540    PRINT "CØMPET EFFECTIVENESS:% YR1, YR2, YR3";
5550    INPUT X[27],X[28],X[29]
5560    LET S2=(X[42]*X[41]+X[6]/100*(100-X[41]))/100
5570    LET S[1]=S2*X[8]*(100+X[24])/(100+X[27])
5580    LET S[2]=S2*X[8]*(100+X[25])/(100+X[28])
5590    LET S[3]=S2*X[8]*(100+X[26])/(100+X[29])
5600    GØTØ 1120
6000    REM CANNIBALISATIØN MØDEL
6010    IF G$[1,1]="Y" THEN 6080
6020    IF Z2=1 THEN 6070
6030    PRINT "GRØWTH WITH CØMPETN:% YR1, YR2, YR3";
6040    INPUT X[24],X[25,X[26]
6050    PRINT "CØMPET EFFECTIVENESS:% YR1, YR2, YR3";
6060    INPUT X[27],X[28],X[29]
6070    LET S2=X[6]/100
6080    IF Z2=1 THEN 6150
6090    PRINT "MKT GRØWTH (NØ MAXWELL HØUSE): % YR2, YR3";
6100    INPUT X[30],X[31]
6110    PRINT "% FRØM MAXWELL HØUSE, % FRØM INSTANT";
6120    INPUT X[32],X[33]
6130    PRINT "% ADVERTISING CUT";
6140    INPUT X[34]
6150    LET U[1]=S2*X[8]*(100+X[24]-X[27])/100
6160    LET U[2]=S2*X[8]*(100+X[25]-X[28]*(100+X[30])/100)/100
```

```
6170    LET U[3]=S2*X[8]*(100+X[26]-X[29]*(100+X[31])/100)/100
6180    IF X[33]<0 THEN 6220
6190    LET W1=.503*.3*(100-X[33])/100*(2.5-.7*X[34]/100)
6200    LET W2=(.503*.3*X[33]/100+.249*.7)*(2-.7*X[34]/100)
6210    GØTØ 6240
6220    LET W1=(.503*.3+.249*.7*(-X[33]))/100)*(2.5-.7*X[34]/100)
6230    LET W2=.249*.7*(100+X[33])/100*(2-.7*X[34]/100)
6240    LET T9=(100-X[32])/100*(W1+W2)
6250    LET X[17]=U[1]*T9
6260    LET X[18]=U[2]*T9
6270    LET X[19]=U[3]*T9
6280    IF Z2=1 THEN 1500
6290    GØTØ 1230
9999    END
```

8